P9-CFN-039

VOICES OF NORTHERN IRELAND

BOOKS BY CAROLYN MEYER

Nonfiction

VOICES OF SOUTH AFRICA:
Growing Up in a Troubled Land

THE MYSTERY OF THE ANCIENT MAYA
WITH CHARLES GALLENKAMP

AMISH PEOPLE:
Plain Living in a Complex World

THE CENTER:
From a Troubled Past to a New Life

THE BREAD BOOK:
All About Bread and How to Make It

MASK MAGIC

Fiction

ELLIOTT & WIN

C. C. POINDEXTER

EULALIA'S ISLAND

THE SUMMER I LEARNED ABOUT LIFE

THE LUCK OF TEXAS McCOY

VOICES OF NORTHERN IRELAND

GROWING · UP · IN A · TROUBLED · LAND

BY CAROLYN MEYER

GULLIVER BOOKS
HARCOURT BRACE JOVANOVICH
SAN DIEGO AUSTIN ORLANDO

Library of Congress Cataloging-in-Publication Data
Meyer, Carolyn.
Voices of Northern Ireland.
"Gulliver books."
Bibliography: p.
Includes index.
Summary: The author relates her visit to Northern Ireland where she interviewed Protestants and Catholics and recorded their feelings growing up in a country torn apart by religious and political conflict.
1. Northern Ireland—Social life and customs.
2. Northern Ireland—Description and travel—1981–
3. Children—Northern Ireland. 4. Meyer, Carolyn—Journeys—Northern Ireland. [1. Northern Ireland—Social conditions. 2. Northern Ireland—Description and travel] I. Title
DA990.U46M46 1987 941.60824 87-199
ISBN 0-15-200635-4

Designed by Francesca Moira Smith
Printed in the United States of America
First edition A B C D E

To Michael McHugh
and
To the memory of Eamonn McMillan

CONTENTS

CONTENTS

Maps appear on pages x–xi, 18, 64, and 98.

Miles
0
40
0
40
Kms.
ULSTER
NORTHERN
IRELAND
Donegal
ULSTER
CONNACHT
IRELAND
Galway
DUBLIN
LEINSTER
Limerick
Waterford
MUNSTER
Cork
St. George's Channel
Atlantic Ocean
Londonderry
FERMANAGH
NORTHERN IRELAND
©A·Karl/J·Kemp 1987

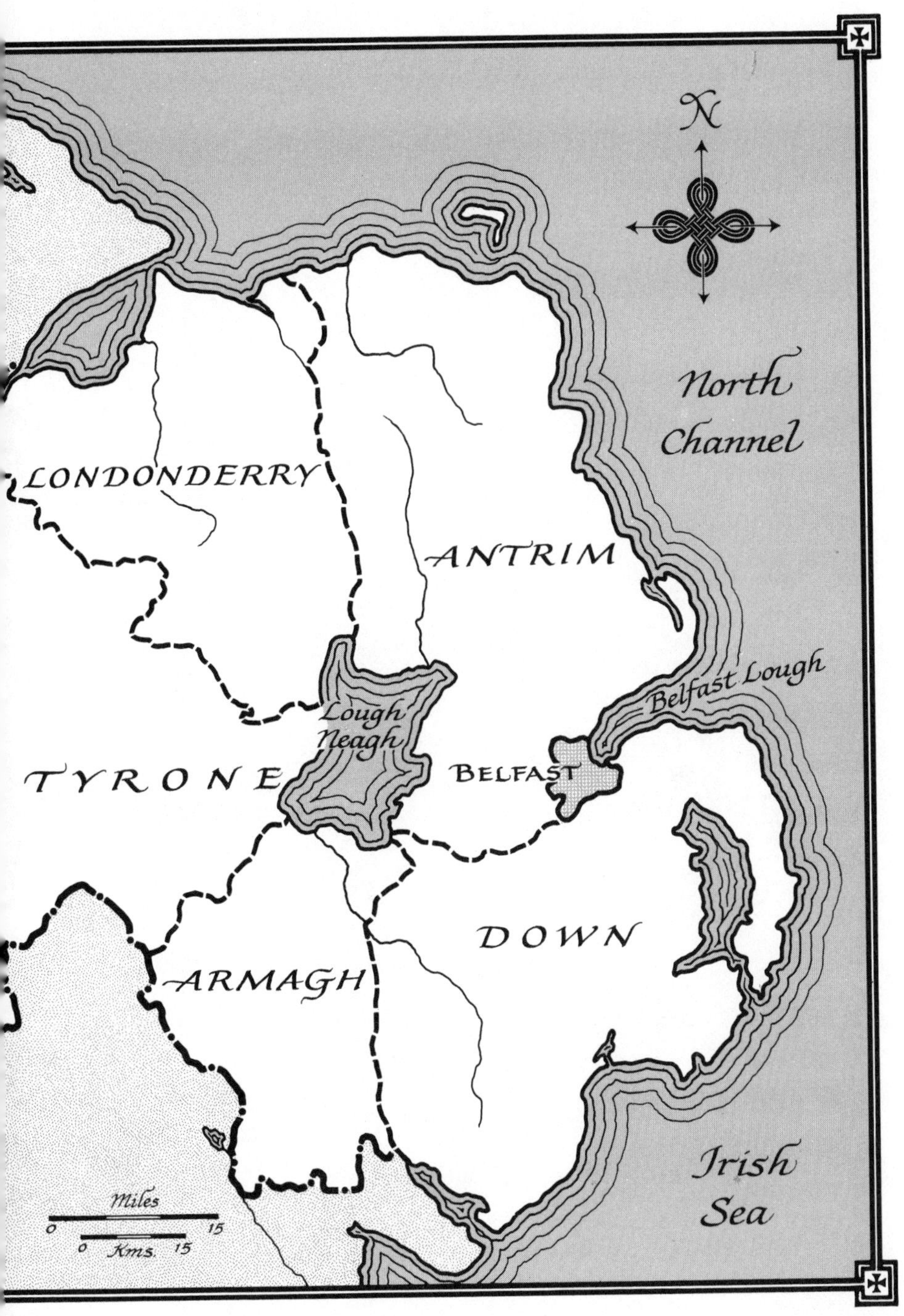
N
North Channel
LONDONDERRY
ANTRIM
Belfast Lough
Lough Neagh
TYRONE
BELFAST
DOWN
ARMAGH
Irish Sea
Miles
0
15
0
Kms.
15

PROLOGUE:
ROMEO AND JULIET IN BELFAST

Ian and Maureen

They had been married for a couple of months and gazed at each other fondly, radiating the special happiness of newlyweds. They had their private, teasing jokes. But they admitted that getting to this stage had not been easy—and their life together might not get easier. Their families warned them there would be trouble. Sometimes the pressure had been too much for them; once they broke up, didn't see each other for several months, couldn't stand it, got back together again. That was when they decided to get married, no matter what.

"God is on our side," Maureen says.

God may be on their side, but Ian is Protestant and Maureen is Catholic in a country where Protestants and Catholics have hated each other for hundreds of years. It is a country where everybody is identified as one or the other and where most people live in areas belonging exclusively to one group or the other. Because of the way things are in Northern Ireland, the marriage of Ian and Maureen is a Romeo-and-Juliet affair. Their wedding ended a long and difficult time of soul-searching for both of them. Now that they have made their commitment, they are beginning a life that will be filled with problems and conflicts, a life that carries with it the potential for tragedy. To make matters more complicated, Ian is a policeman and the potential target of violence from both sides.

Ian resembles a big teddy bear with cinnamon-colored hair and hazel eyes. Maureen is tiny, dark-haired, blue-eyed. She grew up in Ardoyne, a working-class Catholic section of Belfast; Ian's home was in Dunmurry, exclusively Protestant. Maureen is a teacher and Ian a member of the Community Relations Branch of the Royal Ulster Constabulary (RUC), the police of Northern Ireland. They now live in one of the "mixed" areas of Belfast, where they are not bothered by their middle-class neighbors because of their mixed marriage.

On Sunday mornings Ian drives out to Dunmurry to attend services at the Church of Ireland with his mother. Usually referred to as C of I (written "CofI"), the Church of Ireland is part of the Anglican church, like the Church of England in Great Britain and Canada and the Episcopal Church in the United States. Maureen would like to go to mass in Ardoyne with her mother and the brothers and sisters still living there, but she's afraid to go to a Catholic area known to be dominated by the IRA, the Irish Republican Army. So she attends church near home with Seamus (pronounced SHAY-muhs, the Irish version of James) and Bridie McHugh, the couple who had arranged for us to meet.

We talked in the lobby of a Belfast hotel in the University area where I was staying, a mixed neighborhood where we were safe enough. They said they had only an hour to spend with me, so we talked fast.

"Why are you afraid to go home to Ardoyne?" I asked Maureen. "What do you think will happen to you?"

"I'm afraid somebody will shoot me."

"Why would somebody shoot you?"

"Because I married a Prod. And even worse than that, because I married a policeman."

"I can't go there *ever,*" Ian said. "I used to be assigned to that neighborhood, and all the kids recognize me."

There's a blue minibus parked outside their house, they said, used to transport mixed groups of Catholic and Protestant children to swimming pools, to weekend camps, to specially organized discos and quiz competitions. Ian described how he drives through Catholic neighborhoods, collecting Catholic kids, and then waits at the edge of the Protestant area for Protestant kids to come out to him. It would not be safe to drive through a Protestant area with a busload of Catholics; the Protestants would be enraged, and the Catholics would be scared to death. And the same holds for Protestants in a Catholic area.

Ian and Maureen met when they were both involved in working with young people, he through the RUC, she through her school. The Catholic school in which she taught had given her a year off for special community projects, but when she became engaged to Ian, her old teaching position was suddenly made "redundant"—meaning that they didn't need her any more, and she was out of a job when the year was up.

Maureen went to the principal of the school, a nun, and demanded an explanation. "It's because of your personal situation," the nun told her. Hurt and angry, Maureen took legal action to force the school administrators to admit publicly why they had fired her, and although she knew she was entitled to compensation, she stopped short of pressing for that. She was afraid of repercussions, retaliation of some sort.

The Community Relations Branch of the RUC where Ian has worked since he first joined the force has been eliminated in many areas where the situation is particularly tense. The police have become a hated organization, the target of violence from both Protestants and Catholics. Ian had already been transferred from an earlier post because he was "too good," too successful at getting mixed groups of Protestant and Catholic children together. He was the target of anger from both sides; the transfer was for his own safety. People like Ian live on a knife-edge.

I kept an eye on the clock in the hotel lobby. They had told me they were free only from seven o'clock until "half eight," when they were due to visit friends. It was already past eight o'clock. "I'll ring them up and tell them we'll come next week," Ian told Maureen. When he came back he said, "Let's go out to McHughs' instead. It'll be a good crack." ("Crack" means *fun* or *good time* in Northern Ireland. "It'll be a good crack," somebody says, or "The crack was brilliant.")

We stopped on the way to buy food to take along, and while Ian was in the shop I asked Maureen if she worried about him—if she was afraid he'd be killed or their house would be bombed. It happens to policemen all the time in Northern Ireland.

"I'm not scared because he's not. He won't even carry a gun, and all the RUC men are issued guns. But the night he was an hour late coming home I was half-crazy with worry."

When Ian got back into the car, again the conversation drifted to the subject of their marriage. *He* said the big wedding was her idea. *She* said he was the one who insisted. "All I wanted was the crack," Ian protested, "a big party with my friends."

It may have been a good crack for Ian, but it was a lot of work for Maureen—choosing the color scheme, coordinating the flowers, arranging for the pictures, the cars, the food, the outfits. Their parents were surprised that they didn't get married the summer before, while they were both in the United States as leaders of a youth exchange program. It might have saved them a lot of trouble, and not just in choosing the style of the bridesmaids' dresses.

One of the first stumbling blocks they had encountered was where they would be married and who would perform the ceremony. Naturally the ceremony would be in a Catholic church, and by a Catholic priest—they would not be married in the eyes of Maureen's church if it were otherwise. But they wanted to have Ian's CofI minister assist in the ceremony. Catholic and CofI worship services are remarkably similar, partly because the Anglican church is a centuries-old split from the Roman Catholic church. But although traditions are similar, the division between the two is deep. Ian's minister said that he'd be glad to perform the ceremony, but the CofI bishop refused permission.

The reason for the CofI bishop's refusal reflects one of the major issues dividing the churches: how children of the marriage are to be reared. The Catholic church requires that the Catholic partner promise to raise the children as Catholics. It's not a debatable issue. The CofI bishop who refused to allow Ian's minister to take part in the ceremony argued that the attitude of the Catholic church was "unfair," and he would not cooperate.

But for Maureen who made the promise and for Ian who agreed, the issue has not been resolved. "We still haven't decided," Maureen said, "even though I promised."

Although mixed marriages are unusual, they're not unheard of. Generally children are raised in the religion of the parent with the strongest church ties, regardless of what promises were made. But that wouldn't work with these two, both of whom seem equally committed to their faiths, or at least to their churches. So they keep trying to come up with the perfect compromise, something that is absolutely "fair."

"We thought of raising the girls Catholic and the boys Protestant," Maureen said. "But what if there were more girls than boys, or the other way around? That wouldn't be *fair*."

"Then we thought of alternating, one child Catholic, one Protestant, but which one would you start with?" Ian said. "Even if we tossed a coin for the first one, we'd have to have an even number. And suppose we had only one? That wouldn't be *fair*."

"I know Ian would love to have children, and I would too," Maureen said, "but I'm terrified of getting pregnant. Then we'd have to decide." Even though birth control is against the doctrine of her church, she takes the Pill. It makes her sick—probably, she admitted, because she feels guilty about it. With the birth of a baby the problems that divide them would come to a head—"Just the way my mother said it would. Just the way Ian's mother told him it would."

We had pulled up in front of the McHughs' house when another subject surfaced. "It makes me sad," Maureen said, "that I can't share my faith with Ian, something that's so important to me." Ian said the same thing was true from his side.

With an outsider's view of things, I offered some advice. I thought they needed to find a different approach. What did they know about each other's beliefs? Did they realize how much alike they were in many of their traditions? "You're talking about the same God and the same Jesus Christ. Why not look for ways to integrate the two great traditions?" They stared at me with astonishment. Exploring similarities is not the way people think here; harping on differences is.

I met Ian and Maureen Hall just before I left Northern Ireland, after nearly six weeks of meeting people and listening to their stories. And I saw in Ian and Maureen, who love each other dearly, all the symptoms that make their country such a sad and hopeless place. There is nothing in their history, nothing in their culture, that teaches them creative ways to work through a problem. They believe that if somebody wins, then somebody else has to lose. Compromise in Northern Ireland is seen only in terms of what might be lost, not in terms of what can be gained. There is relentless emphasis on the negative, and this negativity shows up in political slogans and graffiti: ULSTER SAYS NO. The entire country seems to be disfigured with the slogan of the Protestant refusal to compromise. (Ulster is another name for Northern Ireland.) In exasperation I grumbled to a journalist, "Does anybody in this country ever say YES to anything?"

"Well," he said, "I have a tee shirt that says ULSTER SAYS MAYBE."

Northern Ireland, comprising the northeast quarter of the island of Ireland, is a country that focuses on its past, rather than on its future. Someone told the story of flying to Northern Ireland; the pilot announced over the intercom, "We are now landing in Belfast. Turn your watches back three hundred years."

Three centuries may not be enough. The conflict reflected in the marriage of Ian and Maureen carries religious labels, but "Protestant" and "Catholic" are simply convenient ways of identifying people with different backgrounds—cultural, political, and economic, as well as religious. These backgrounds are part of their histories, separate but intertwined. The Catholics of Northern Ireland, the powerless and economically inferior minority, are descended from the original inhabitants of Ireland. Many of them want independence from the United Kingdom, of which Northern Ireland is a part. All want a stake in the government, equal opportunity in jobs and housing, a piece of the economic pie. The Protestants, descendants of sixteenth-century colonizers from England and Scotland, own most of the land and businesses in Northern Ireland, hold most of the power, look to the United Kingdom to help them maintain that control, and desperately fear the loss of it.

Ireland—the island—lies west of Great Britain, separated from it by a narrow strip of water, the Irish Sea. Ireland is about 140 miles wide and 225 miles from north to south—32,598 square miles, smaller than the state of Indiana. The island has been a target for invaders for 2,000 years. The first were bands of Celts (pronounced KELTS) who arrived about two centuries before the birth of Christ.

Early in its history the island was roughly divided into provinces, which were ruled by chieftains. At the end of the eighth century, Viking warriors swept down from the north. Some stayed in Ireland and built trading towns along the coasts; Dublin began as one of those early towns.

In the twelfth century the English king Henry II sent an army across the Irish Sea to subdue the Celts. Many of these invaders also decided to stay and were eventually absorbed into the Celtic culture. These are the forebears of present-day Catholics in Ireland.

In succeeding centuries the English attempted again and again to get the Irish under their thumbs, and the Irish tried again and again to get out from under. King Henry VIII tried—making himself King of Ireland—and failed. Elizabeth I tried, and put down several rebellions, confiscating land belonging to the rebel leaders and handing it over to her loyal Protestant supporters. In the end, she too failed. King James I tried, systematically planting Scottish and English Protestants in the northern quarter of Ireland, the province of Ulster.

In the seventeenth century Oliver Cromwell was dispatched to Ireland to punish another generation of rebels, which he did promptly and viciously, seizing whatever land was left. Along came James II, a Catholic, who was forced to give up the English throne to his son-in-law, William of Orange, a Protestant from the Netherlands. James showed up in Ireland at the head of a rebelling army. Then new King William arrived with *his* army and soundly defeated James II at the Battle of the Boyne. The year was 1690, a date that rings proudly in the ears of the Protestants of Northern Ireland.

The gulf widened between colonizer and native, between rebel and conqueror. By the end of the eighteenth century, revolution was in the air—in France and in the American colonies. The Irish rebelled again, and failed. By this time the English were thoroughly sick of the rebellious Irish who never won, but never quit trying. In the mid-nineteenth century the potato crop, the main staple of the Irish-Catholic diet, failed for several years in a row, leading to the death of a million people and the emigration of a million more, many to the United States. Rulers came and went; military groups formed and disappeared. In 1916 there was still another futile attempt by the Irish to break free of English rule.

Not everyone wanted to be free of England. Most of the Irish Catholics did, but most of the Protestants, descendants of the early Scottish and English settlers, did not. Soon the Unionists, who insisted on remaining part of the United Kingdom, were fighting the Nationalists, who demanded that Ireland be a free and independent country.

In an attempt to stop the war, the British government divided Ireland in two. The six northeastern counties would remain part of the United Kingdom and be known as Northern Ireland. The other twenty-six counties became the Irish Free State (later becoming Eire, and finally the Republic of Ireland), which is politically independent of the United Kingdom. The division did not end the conflict; it complicated it further by keeping the British involved as a third party between Unionists and Nationalists.

The gulf also widened between the powerful and the powerless, the haves and the have-nots. In the late 1960s, inspired by civil rights activism in the United States, the Catholics of Northern Ireland began a series of demonstrations and marches to protest a long list of grievances, especially in housing and employment. Protestants, with a two-to-one majority, staged counterdemonstrations. This was the beginning of "the Troubles," with bombings and shootings, bloodshed and hatred, and killing of innocent people, Protestants against Catholics, Unionists against Nationalists, loyalists against republicans.

There is no "peace" in Northern Ireland, not as we in the United States understand it. There is only, at times, less violence than at others. But the tension is always there. It has a deep effect on people. I wanted to see what this effect was—especially on the young.

I first thought of going to Northern Ireland late in 1985, when I was working on *Voices of South Africa: Growing Up in a Troubled Land.* I had spent five weeks in South Africa in August and September of that year, talking with people there to find out what it's like to be young in a country torn apart by racial strife. I don't remember precisely what triggered the idea of Northern Ireland—a newspaper article, perhaps—but in that early intuitive flash I guessed there might be interesting similarities between the two countries.

For as long as anyone can remember, there has been strife in Ireland. Late in 1985 a new agreement between the leaders of the United Kingdom and the Republic of Ireland gave the Republic a say in the affairs of Northern Ireland. This agreement raised tensions again.

During the winter and spring I read about Ireland, both

the Republic and Northern Ireland. I wrote dozens of letters, trying to establish contacts. Not everyone was thrilled at the idea of yet one more American writer coming to poke around, jump to easy conclusions, and offer unwanted advice. Some people refused to help at all, but others did what they could, always cautioning me, not just to watch out for my own safety, but to be mindful of the jeopardy in which I could carelessly involve others.

One of the people I wanted to see was a CofI minister in the Republic who had organized a project to promote understanding between Protestant and Catholic teenagers in the North. I'll call his project "Channels of Peace." When he eventually answered my letter, he was not encouraging:

"The situation in the North here is deteriorating—I was nearly caught in a bomb explosion myself last week, but such happenings do not even raise an eyebrow amongst these wonderfully durable people. The arrival of yet another 'Outsider' wishing to write a book about the Troubles would be unlikely to receive public acclamation. . . . We always proceed with extreme caution—we are involved with people's lives. It would be unthinkable that a letter from you, or any author (for you are not the first to approach me) would immediately produce names and addresses for you to use. You would need first class references, and I would need to have an honest statement as to what good you think your book will produce, and why exactly it is contemplated."

It was not going to be easy. I sent the references he wanted and tried to answer honestly the questions of what good I thought my book would produce and why I wanted to do it—to bring readers a better understanding of people in Northern Ireland and the problems they face, hoping this will help readers to examine their own values and their own prejudices.

By the time I left home on May 15, 1986, I had a long list

of possible contacts, many of them official agencies of the government but few sounding like Real People. All I needed were a couple of names, and I didn't have them.

The morning I arrived in Ireland I called the reluctant minister and told him I'd be in his town the next day. He said he'd meet the train.

Next I bought a stout and ugly pair of shoes made in England guaranteed to keep my feet dry during the endless rain characteristic of Irish weather. The following day I stood in a downpour on a railway platform somewhere in the middle of Ireland, water leaking up through the soles of my new shoes. Eventually a man in a clerical collar drove up in a rattletrap car. "Where's your luggage?" he demanded.

"This is it." I had a garment bag over my shoulder, a little carry-on bag at my feet.

"I usually have to put the luggage rack on the car when I meet Americans," he said, still not smiling. I thought I might like him after all.

He showed me around his town, which didn't take long, and took me to his church, a great stone edifice on a hill. Ninety-five percent of the population of the Republic is Roman Catholic; only a small percent belong to the Church of Ireland. The building is large, but the congregation is small. He turned on the electric fire in the living room of the ancient rectory, centuries of dampness and chill forever in its thick stone walls, and his wife left us a tray of tea and buttered bread. I began to thaw out. I did like him after all. I thought he probably liked me. After two hours of pleasant conversation without any mention of why I was there, he dropped me off at the guest house where he had reserved me a room. He recommended a restaurant and said he'd look for me in church the next morning.

It was a long walk out to the church on the hill, but I got there early. The minister, arrayed in his vestments for the service, came down the aisle and handed me a prayer book. Inside the prayer book was an envelope, and inside the envelope was a brief list of people who would help me when I got to Belfast. I didn't talk to him again; he disappeared immediately after the service to visit tiny congregations in other towns. A couple of days later I arrived in Belfast with the minister's list, ready to begin.

There is a great deal of hostility in Northern Ireland toward foreign journalists, who many believe get rich on the misery of others. I had to convince the doubters that I was not one of those, that I don't work on assignment for a newspaper, a magazine, or a television network; that I write books for teenagers, a different kind of work altogether. I told those who asked that I write these books because it is what I feel I'm *supposed* to be doing. It doesn't make me rich.

I don't do formal interviews, take notes, or use a tape recorder, but I do keep detailed journals of people I've met, conversations I've had, feelings I've experienced. I carry a little notebook in case I need to jot down somebody's name or a specific bit of information. I try to make my visit an opportunity for an exchange, not just a chance for a story. I am there to listen, to discuss, to develop friendships, to show that I care about the people I meet. I enter into their lives, and I allow them into mine. When I leave, I want people to feel that I have given them something of value, that our time together enriched their lives, as it did mine.

I spent about half my time in Belfast, making that a base from which to travel, depending on a combination of trains, buses, taxis, rental cars, and the kindness of people willing to give me a lift. I visited all but one of the six counties of Northern Ireland, usually staying in B&B's—clean, cheap bed-and-breakfast places. I was in country towns, mill towns, and small cities, and I met as many different kinds of people as I could—Catholics and Protestants in more or less equal number, people for whom unemployment was a way of life and others who worked hard and lived well, people of all ages. I played with babies, visited schools and churches and youth centers, talked with senior citizens, went to concerts and discos. I tried to get a feel for the place.

I was not happy in Northern Ireland. Part of it was the weather, so awful that people boast about its awfulness. It rained every day for a month—from mid-May to mid-June, the one time of the year that is supposed to be sunny. The rain was more than a depressing inconvenience; crops were rotting in the fields.

And I had wet feet. I seemed always to be standing somewhere in the rain. At night I draped my clothes over a radiator and hoped they'd be dry by morning. Friends took me on a drive south of Belfast to see the Mourne Mountains, said to be very beautiful, but even when the rain stopped briefly the mountains were shrouded in fog. The rain was always a safe topic of conversation. "They say that when you can see the Mournes, it's going to rain," a taxi driver told me. "And when you can't see the Mournes, it's raining."

But it wasn't just the weather. It was the distrust, the suspicion, the anger always simmering just below the surface. People talked about "having a good crack," but they seldom seemed really to be having fun. How could they? They were too busy deciding whether a stranger is Catholic or Protestant, and if it was "the other one," then bracing for trouble, for dislike, maybe for anger or hatred, possibly for violence. It has been going on for hundreds of years, and it seems likely that it will go on for hundreds more.

I had many mixed feelings about Northern Ireland. It reminded me of a couple caught in a bad marriage, neither willing to allow the other a way out, afraid of losing something, yet too stubborn to change, too angry and unforgiving to make it work. It's tiresome to be around such a couple—even when you like both people. I got tired, too, of the obsession with religion—because that's not what the Troubles are about. There were times when I simply wanted to go home. But more than I wanted to leave, I wanted to learn—to try to figure out what really goes on.

I did find many similarities between Northern Ireland and South Africa. In both countries there is a conflict between natives (blacks in South Africa, Celtic Irish Catholics in Northern Ireland) and colonizers (whites in South Africa, Scots and English in Northern Ireland). The colonizers need to feel superior to the natives of the land they have taken over—land the colonizers believe they have improved with their own industry and intelligence—and to see the natives as inferior.

And so they create stereotypes. White South Africans describe blacks as lazy, superstitious, stupid, hard to educate, prone to drink too much and to fight among themselves. "They breed like rabbits," I heard whites say of blacks—a significant comment, because the minority white colonizers fear being overwhelmed, physically and culturally, by blacks who outnumber them four to one. Protestants in Northern Ireland describe Catholics as lazy, superstitious, stupid, hard to educate, prone to drink too much and to fight among themselves. "They breed like rabbits," I heard Protestants say of Catholics. Although Protestants outnumber Catholics two to one in Northern Ireland, if Catholics in all of Ireland, the North and the Republic, joined together, they would then significantly outnumber the Protestants. The response in both countries by those in control is to refuse to change. This angers those out of power. Tension mounts and violence flares.

Violence in Northern Ireland is a part of the fabric of life. As a visitor I never felt that I was in danger. Most ordinary citizens didn't seem to worry about their safety either. But every few days the newspapers would carry reports of some new incident: a police inspector shot dead by IRA gunmen as he walked his dog, police officers injured at a Loyalist parade, plastic bullets fired at rioting youths, a man murdered in a border town by the IRA. Most of the violence is between Catholic and Protestant terrorist groups or is directed against the police, but sometimes it's against ordinary people: a young woman was killed and her husband wounded by a Loyalist gang because of their mixed marriage.

I was acutely aware of my own limitations. I was an outsider in Northern Ireland, as I had been in South Africa, and I'm certain there were things I saw incorrectly, didn't catch at all, or interpreted wrongly. There were things I didn't have time to do (the Girl Guides' campout and cook-off, for instance), places I didn't go (I never did visit County Fermanagh), people I didn't have a chance to meet.

Home again at the end of six weeks, I plunged into writing this book. An immediate problem was how to protect the privacy of a generous handful of people whose friendship and trust became important to me. I remembered a line from the Channels of Peace minister's letter: "We always proceed with extreme caution—we are involved with people's lives." For that reason I proceeded with extreme caution, too, and changed the names and altered the personal details of most people and many places in this book.

A greater challenge was to create a mosaic of my own experiences and feelings against a background of reading—history, politics, novels, and poetry—to present a picture of life in this sad, troubled country that would contribute to a better understanding of the people of Northern Ireland, and, ultimately, to a better understanding of ourselves.

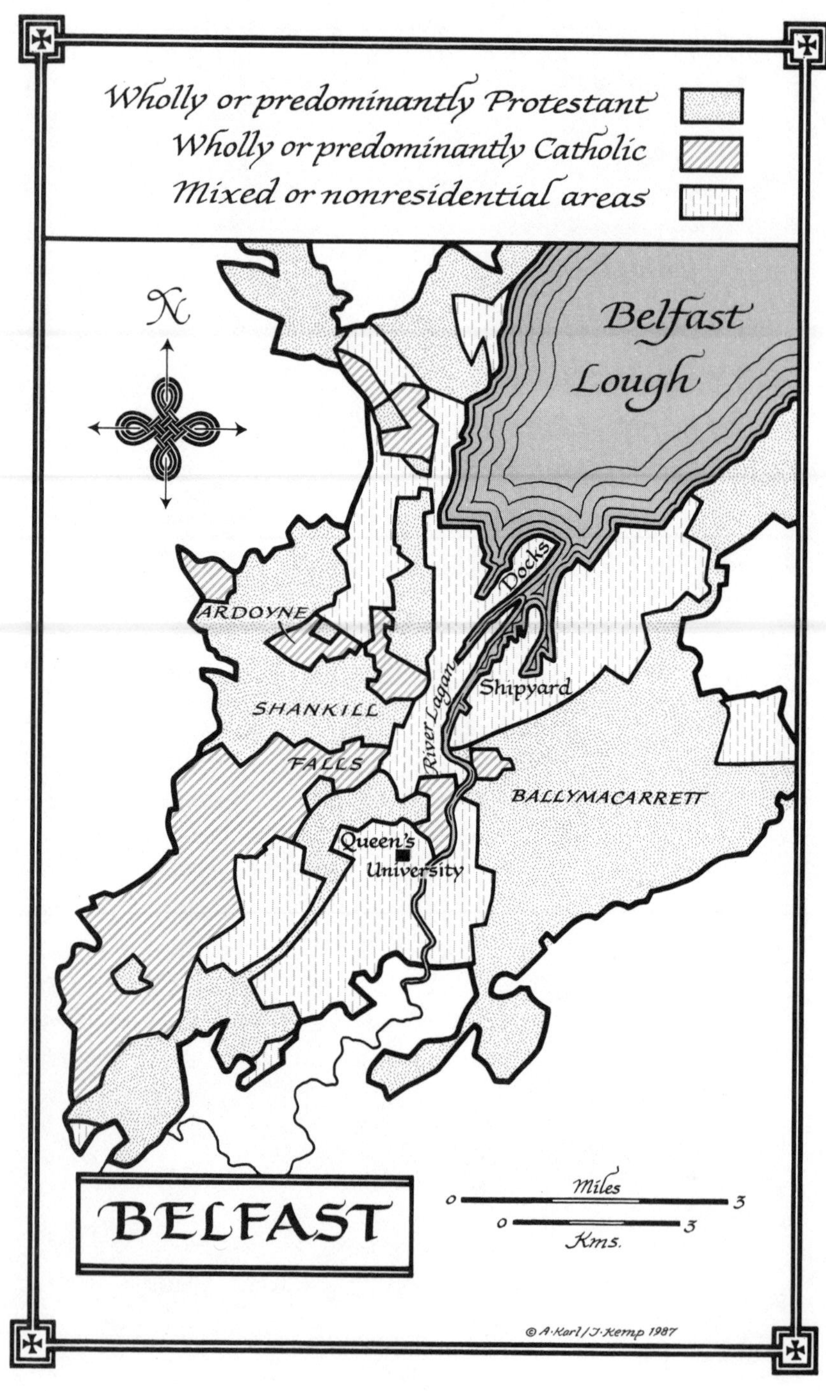

Wholly or predominantly Protestant
Wholly or predominantly Catholic
Mixed or nonresidential areas
N
Belfast Lough
Docks
ARDOYNE
Shipyard
SHANKILL
River Lagan
FALLS
BALLYMACARRETT
Queen's University
BELFAST
Miles
0
3
0
3
Kms.
© A·Karl / J·Kemp 1987

I

CATHOLIC BELFAST: THERE ARE NO DREAMS

Seamus McHugh

Seamus and Bridie McHugh make room for strangers. They took me along to meet their relatives, invited me over for meals, put me in touch with people like their neighbors Ian and Maureen Hall, explained things to me, listened to my stories, cheered me up when I got discouraged. They became my family.

Seamus headed the list given me by the minister in the South. Seamus and Bridie (nickname for Bridget) are both from large families, their brothers and sisters scattered across Ireland and America. Childless themselves, they are surrounded by children: the ones they teach; the nieces and nephews who always seem to be having birthdays or first communions, graduating, or getting married; and the kids in the neighborhood who come by to visit.

The McHughs are middle-class Catholics who worked hard to achieve that status. They live in a pleasant house with a piano and long shelves of books. There is a tiny backyard (they call it a garden), and a garage for their fairly new car.

This sets them a world apart from the Catholics who live in West Belfast, on the other side of town. Owning a house is an upper-middle-class privilege in Northern Ireland. Most "working-class" people—we'd call them blue-collar in the United States—both Catholics and Protestants, rent homes in public housing projects known as "estates." Narrow brick row houses have a front door opening onto the street and a backyard with a coalbin and a high wall to cut it off from the neighbors' yard. Usually there are two bedrooms upstairs and a toilet downstairs, at the back of the house—tight quarters for big families.

The estates are controlled by Protestant-dominated housing boards, and for a long time discrimination in housing was one of the major Catholic grievances. Sometimes slums were cleared away to make room for high-rise buildings, like Divis Flats (apartments are called "flats") near the center of Belfast. But the buildings have become vertical slums, no better than the housing they replaced, with the poverty and wretchedness and high crime rate usually associated with slums.

With a stiff-legged walk that earned him the nickname "Humpy" from his students, Seamus teaches in a high school in a Catholic working-class neighborhood surrounded by middle-class Protestants. Identifiable as Catholic by its saint's name, it is an intermediate school for boys. "Intermediate" means its students failed the qualifying exam that would have gotten them into more prestigious, academically oriented grammar schools.

Seamus teaches a class of boys who normally would be "school leavers"—dropouts. Students who turn sixteen before August 31 are allowed to leave school in May; those with later birthdays must stay until Easter of the next year. Many pupils who are not good students decide to leave. But the job situation is so desperate, so impossible, that courses have been designed to keep them in school for as long as possible—and off the unemployment rolls, called "the dole" in England and "the Bru" (probably short for Bureau) in Northern Ireland.

Seamus has managed to keep a class of potential leavers coming for a course in government. Four of them met us in the library, where we sat around a table stacked with paperback novels by Irish writers. The novels looked interesting, but the boys don't care much about reading and claim that they never open a book.

Joe is a lanky boy with reddish hair and freckles and a crooked, friendly smile. Paul is tall and well muscled with dark hair curling on his neck and a need to be the center of attention. Gerald, square-jawed with piercing blue eyes, didn't say much, but when he did, he spoke directly. Charles, a thin-faced boy, slouched with his head on the table, apparently paying no attention; he was the one who went to fetch tea and a plate of gingersnaps.

Seamus made the introductions and stayed around for a while, translating for me when necessary their rapid Belfast speech, the vowels stretched out and most of the consonants lost along the way. A local humorist built his reputation making jokes about "Norn Iron," the Belfast pronunciation of Northern Ireland.

Only one of the four had a job prospect; Charles, the nonparticipator, would begin working soon for a sheet metal company, a job he got through someone his father knows.

"It's all in who you know," Paul said. They all agreed.

"What kinds of jobs are you looking for?" I asked them.

Shrugs. "Just a job." "Any kind of job." "Someplace where I can make money."

"But if you could have any kind of job at all, what would it be?"

The four of them stared at me as though I were completely

daft. Unemployment in Northern Ireland is the highest in Europe, and these boys, nearing their seventeenth birthdays, represent the largest group of unemployed. The figure is sometimes quoted at 30 percent unemployment in Belfast, higher in some of the Catholic neighborhoods; in the worst areas something like *80 percent* of the young men from sixteen to twenty-five have no jobs.

In an attempt to give young people some marketable skills that will increase their chances of finding work, the government has pumped millions of dollars into YTP, the Youth Training Program. Boys and girls sign up for a course, which runs a year or more, and are paid a small salary—a bit more than they would collect on the Bru. They learn skills like carpentry, welding, bricklaying, catering, industrial weaving. But the program has gotten a lot of criticism.

"It's boring," Seamus's students said. "And useless. You go through all that and there are still no jobs."

Signs on Belfast buses urge young people to register for the YTP; officials quote high employment figures for YTP graduates, but no one believes those figures. There are simply not enough jobs.

It has been this way for a long time. For many men, unemployment is chronic; they have lived all their lives on the Bru, and their sons will live all *their* lives on the Bru. In that "culture of nonwork," it is all they know. There are no dreams.

"I want a life of adventure," Paul, the big mouth, said, but he couldn't explain what he meant.

Seamus asked Paul to tell me about his family, and suddenly Big Mouth grew quiet. The library was silent, except for the shuffling outside in the hall as classes changed. Fifteen months ago, Paul said haltingly, a gang of gunmen burst into his home and "opened up"—began firing—wounding his younger sister. Paul wasn't home at the time; in fact there were no men in the house, just Paul's mother and sisters and a cousin. Apparently the gunmen were looking for someone else.

"Who was it?" I asked.

"UDA," Paul said—the Ulster Defence Association, an illegal Protestant paramilitary organization parallel to the IRA.

"You *think* it was the UDA," Seamus corrected. "You don't know for sure."

His sister recovered physically from the shooting, although she will be permanently scarred. "But she's having a hard time getting over it. So's me mum. We moved to a different house. She couldn't stand it there anymore."

Gerald said that his older brother had been "lifted," detained for questioning, regarding an attack on some invading Prods in which one was beaten to death. Joe mentioned his two uncles killed in the Troubles, but he didn't know them and claimed not to be affected by their deaths. "It don't mean much unless it happens to *you*, right in your own family, like."

I produced a small Belfast map, and Paul sketched the outlines of their Catholic neighborhood on it. They laughed and boasted about how they beat up Prods who come into their turf intending to beat *them* up, but I was not sure if the laughter meant bravado or nervousness. "We control the bridges," Joe said. "The Prods have to get by us to get from East Belfast."

That strategic location would be important during the "marching season" in July and August, the traditional time for Protestants to hassle Catholics, while parading through their neighborhoods in the traditional black bowler hats and orange sashes that mark them as members of the Orange Order. They beat their monstrous drums, sing and play anti-Catholic songs, and sometimes get into fights that balloon into riots, violence, and bloodshed.

Seamus left us to go teach another class, and the conversation quickly turned to girls. Paul fancies himself a ladies' man, a "killer." Did I think American girls would like him? Maybe some would want a pen pal? He'd write to them, and they'd invite him over to visit, and they'd all fall down at his feet, right? Maybe he could get a job in America. Marry a rich girl. Something like that is possible in America, isn't it? Nothing is possible here.

When the girls from the sister school next door were dismissed, we watched them pass the window on the way to their buses. "Millies," Paul said scornfully, a term referring to the workers in the linen mills, once Belfast's major industry, but no longer. He insisted that these girls in Catholic school uniforms were raunchy punks with foul mouths and tattoos on their forearms. They looked like convent girls to me.

The boys were curious and doubtful about the fact that people in other parts of the world are interested in Northern Ireland. "Why do Americans want to come to Ireland?" they wondered. "Why do they want to go to Europe? What could be so interesting about that?"

The dismissal bell rang and the boys bolted. Seamus intercepted them and tried to coax them into inviting me to visit their homes that weekend, to meet their parents. They agreed, to please him, but I was not surprised when the invitations failed to materialize.

Seamus gave lifts to two of the teachers who live in his neighborhood. I sat in the backseat with Elizabeth, that rare item, a female teacher in a Catholic boys' school. Elizabeth wanted to know about the books I've written, and especially about my trip to South Africa.

"Were you horrified by what you saw?"

"No—not horrified. *Upset* is probably closer to it."

"But you were able to see the truth." It was not a question.

I had to say no again. "The truth is often complex. My

sympathies are with the Blacks, but sometimes with the Whites as well."

She was clearly disappointed with that answer and asked no more questions. She wanted simple truths, and I couldn't give them to her. I was also discovering that the truth is no more simple in Northern Ireland than it was in South Africa.

Ardoyne

My afternoon with Seamus's students in no way prepared me for a similar type of school in Ardoyne, a poor, working-class, Catholic neighborhood of West Belfast. Someone had given me the name of a teacher. I took a taxi to the entrance of the school, where a couple of boys were on the lookout for me and led me inside. The teacher shook my hand, escorted me to a room with about eight teenage boys, and left me there.

He had picked boys between fifteen and sixteen, although some looked younger. All of them favored tight black stovepipe pants, pointy black shoes, white socks. Some wore shirts and ties with sweaters or scruffy jackets. Their hair was fairly short; a few had stud or loop earrings. One resembled Sylvester Stallone; another looked like a choir boy on a Christmas card. Three younger boys sat back and said nothing, one of the older ones stayed fairly low-key, but the remaining four were smart guys. I couldn't understand a word they said, and they complicated the problem by all talking at once. They pretended to ignore me, cracking unintelligible jokes among themselves—jokes I probably wouldn't get anyway—and roughhousing.

"*Ahem*. I'd like to begin with introductions, and maybe you can tell me a little about yourselves, how old you are. . . ."

A lame beginning. They barely interrupted their horsing

around to tell me their names. Their accents were so strong I couldn't make out what they said. One was telling me something that sounded like "have sex in the marnin'." Before I got too shocked I realized he was saying, "half six in the morning," the way the Northern Irish tell time.

There was no order at all, and nothing I tried seemed to work. They were raising hell, being rude, and I had no idea what to do. Finally, thoroughly annoyed, I told them that I was really not interested in continuing like this and I'd just as soon let them go back to their classes.

They settled down some then. Gradually it emerged that the Sylvester Stallone look-alike was going to prison the next week to serve a three- to five-year sentence.

"What for?"

"Hijacking a bus."

He feigned nonchalance, pretending not to care. He's been in jail before, he said, in at thirteen for two years; now he's sixteen and going back. He shrugged it off; "It's not so bad," he said.

His buddies seized on the topic of hijacking buses and regaled me with explicit details of how it's done: the bus is taken, parked crosswise in the road, sprayed with petrol (gasoline), and ignited. This flaming barricade draws the police, and maybe soldiers, whom the hijackers then bash with bricks and stones.

The blond, blue-eyed, pink-cheeked choir boy mentioned his father who was sent to prison for thirteen years when the boy was two. At the time he had a brother five years older and a baby brother; the twins were not yet born when Da was sent off. Now his father is out.

"Why was he sent to prison?"

"I don't know. My older brother knows, but he won't say."

He mentioned the prison, Long Kesh, where men involved in terrorism are sent. I assumed that the father is probably

IRA, maybe the son, too. "Are you involved?" I asked him. He shrugged and looked away. "Does your father try to influence you one way or the other?"

"No," said the choir boy. "Wouldn't do any good if he did."

But suddenly the conversation was open and moving.

They don't particularly dislike Prods, they told me, but they *hate* the Brits. "We want to kill them all," one boy said.

"What do you want, besides getting rid of the British army?"

Freedom, they said. The right to a job and a decent place to live. I wanted to believe they were sincere, but it sounded pat, and this group had me on guard.

They can't imagine what it's like to live in a country where religion is not an issue at all, let alone *the* issue. They mentioned the teachers they trust in this school, and those they don't. Conversation stopped dead when the career counselor walked through the room on the way to his office. I cocked an eyebrow in his direction: *do you trust him*? They shook their heads: *no*.

I tried to start a discussion on civil rights among Blacks and Native-American Indians in the U.S., whose problems are similar to the Catholics' in Northern Ireland, but they were not interested. They asked instead about the Mafia, roughly equivalent to the IRA in the boys' thinking and therefore maybe heroes. They were disappointed at how little I knew on that subject.

Ardoyne is described as "strongly Republican," meaning that many of its residents feel that all Ireland, north and south, should be united into one country. This unification is the primary goal of the IRA—the Irish Republican Army—which was formed in 1919 to attack police and soldiers working for the British in the War of Independence, Ireland's struggle to break free of Great Britain. Declared illegal in the South in 1936, the IRA's fight for a United Independent Republic of Ireland still goes on. The Catholics in Northern Ireland continued to look to the IRA for protection when the police did nothing to stop attacks by Loyalists, Protestants loyal to Great Britain.

In 1970 the IRA split into two groups: the Official IRA in the Republic of Ireland pursues peaceful means for the reunification of Ireland, but in Northern Ireland the Provos, the Provisional IRA, believe in using force to get the British out of the country so that reunification can take place. Some financial support for the Provos comes from the United States, where people of Irish descent sympathize with IRA goals and raise money to finance the means. Some say that IRA terrorism would shrivel up and die in Northern Ireland if U.S. groups stopped the flow of dollars.

The IRA is a powerful force in Ardoyne and other working-class Catholic areas, ruling with an iron hand. For instance, the legal drinking age in Northern Ireland is eighteen, but the IRA won't allow boys to drink until they're twenty-one; they don't want their junior members dulled with alcohol. The reason there is little drug use in the North, the boys said, compared to the South where it is a huge problem, is that the Provos won't permit it. They also won't allow muggings or stealing, the kind of street crime that plagues many American cities.

IRA discipline is swift and harsh. Kneecapping—shooting the offender in one or both kneecaps, and sometimes, in severe cases, in the elbows as well—is the most common punishment. No one under sixteen is kneecapped. Just the threat of it will bring most young delinquents into line in a hurry. Some who have been kneecapped limp for the rest of their lives, in itself a kind of status symbol.

"But," Choir Boy said, "there's still a lot of tar-and-feathering." He mimicked a chicken, flapping his elbows and squawking.

"What do you think of the IRA?" they asked.

I took a look at the group. They *all* could have passed for choir boys at that moment, but I would bet that most of them are involved with the IRA; certainly some of their brothers, fathers, and uncles are or have been. "I can sympathize with the political goals, having Ireland united as one country," I answered cautiously, "but I can't accept terrorist tactics."

Their attention vanished instantly and they began a belching contest. Choir Boy asked me with wide-eyed innocence if I knew how to catch crabs, and they stopped belching to listen to my answer. I was wary: I didn't know if he meant it literally or if he was really talking about pubic lice. I shook my head. He gave me a double-sided explanation with such a straight face that I still do not know if he was serious or if this was a put-on.

Later, when I thought back on that hour, I wasn't sure which parts of the conversation I could take seriously and which were send-ups. Maybe the whole thing was a performance staged for the benefit of an American visitor. On the other hand, it could have been true—the hijacking, the jail sentences—because this is the kind of world they live in.

Sheila O'Brien

"They were spinning a yarn," said Sheila O'Brien, director of a neighborhood youth club. She called over her husband, Richard, and repeated my story of the bus hijacking and the swaggering young man who was now going off to spend a couple of years in jail.

Richard laughed. "Kids often do this to strangers. We had a boy here once who used to tell stories about his mum carrying bombs into shops. It got him attention, all right, but it could have gotten his mum arrested."

"We'd know about it here, if something like that was happening," Sheila said. "Did he say prison? They don't send kids that age to prison. They send them to juvenile detention, and if he had been sent off when he was thirteen they'd have kept him until he was eighteen."

Sheila would know. Sheila is a tall, big-boned woman who organized this youth club in 1971, knocking together two burned-out buildings so that her own young children and the ones they played with would have a place to go. At first she concentrated on sports and games, but as the facilities expanded and the number of people using them increased, so did the range of programs.

I said I thought it was terrific that Richard, a fair-haired man with thick glasses, was also deeply involved in the club. Sheila just smiled. "He wasn't always. At first he was upset. He thought I had enough to do, I should stay home with our kids. We've got six. But then he began to get interested too, and he ended up going to college for four years, studying psychology. Now he's as much into it as I am. He works with the youth, and I do the administrative work, mostly trying to find money. We could both use a bit of time off."

The club opens about 10:30 A.M. Most of the people who come at that time are unemployed youths, over sixteen and on the Bru. School lets out about 3:30, and the schoolchildren come by for an hour before the club closes down at 4:30. It reopens at 7:00 for the biggest crowd of the day and stays open until 10:00 or so. A new community center a few blocks away has a Saturday night disco, and the youth leaders get a break. The club gets most of its funding from the government, which pours vast sums into facilities like this one, to try to relieve the social problems created by unemployment and poverty. About 450 young people show up regularly. There is a small core group that is like "family," and the rest drift between the youth club and the community center.

Sheila led me on a tour, first to the huge gym with a stage for special shows. She opened a closet stuffed with rackets, balls of all kinds, stacks of roller skates. She showed me the big shower rooms. Before many of the houses in the area were bombed or burned out during riots, before masses of people moved away and new housing was built, the old houses had no bathrooms; people bathed in a sink in the kitchen. Until new housing was built, the club was open for people in the community to use the showers.

We passed a Pac-Man machine, but Sheila claimed that it's not the obsession that it is in the United States. At about twenty-five cents a game, it's too expensive for people living on the Bru. Instead most of them play snooker, a kind of billiards. Richard was involved in a game with several of the young men. "You want to have a bit of a yarn with some of them?" she asked. She rounded up a handful of snooker spectators and sent them to a small room decorated with paintings of grotesque figures, clawed creatures, fanged monsters. No one claimed to understand what they were about. A boy in a shabby, black suit jacket spattered with white was slapping paint on the walls, avoiding the monsters.

The four guys, thin, pale-skinned, raggedly dressed, aged seventeen to twenty-two, were unemployed. All have been through YTP projects, one studying bricklaying, another weaving for work in the textile trade, but there are no jobs. Whatever is available is listed on a bulletin board somewhere in the city center, but competition is fierce and all the jobs require experience, which they don't have and can't get. All their fathers are unemployed, too.

They were clearly not much interested in this conversation, and I was casting about for the subject that would hook them, get them to open up a little. They regarded me with curiosity. "You have a funny laugh," one of them said, and I vowed silently not to laugh again in their presence. "Do all Americans talk with their hands?" another asked, catching me in mid-gesture. I shoved my hands in my pockets. "Can you get me a job in America?"

I asked where in the United States they would like to go, probably a dumb question, expecting to hear New York or Boston or Florida, the places the Irish seem to prefer, but instead they named a place I didn't recognize. It turned out to be Elvis Presley's home in Memphis. I did pique their interest momentarily when I mentioned that I live in Albuquerque, New Mexico, where their beloved Northern Ireland World Cup soccer team was at that very moment preparing for the play-offs in Mexico. Soccer is as safe a topic of conversation as the weather, no matter what group you're with.

In the middle of the Albuquerque conversation, Francis, a slightly built fellow in a torn tee shirt, every other tooth missing, left the room abruptly. In a moment he was back, carrying a plump, smiling baby, his three-month-old nephew. It was an incongruous sight, this tough guy tenderly carrying the baby, but he quickly corrected the image. He jammed a pacifier into the baby's mouth and ordered, "Shut the fuck up!" Later the baby's mother, who looked about seventeen, came to collect it.

There's a pattern here, Sheila said; kids leave school at sixteen, and within a year they're married and have a baby, a baby every year after that, even though the husbands have no jobs; nobody has a job. They make out better on the Bru, with government stipends for each child and for housing and furniture and health care and so on, than they would if they both worked. Being unemployed is a life-style.

I wondered about these early marriages in Belfast, while the Irish elsewhere have a reputation for marrying very late, perhaps in their thirties. "It has to do with cycles," she said. "In cities, where unemployment is so high, people live only for the moment. They want their gratifications *now*. Country people are used to longer cycles, waiting for the calf to become a heifer, waiting for crops to grow, waiting for seasons to pass. Country people see things in longer term. They're in no hurry to marry. Here it may be all they have to do."

Father Joseph Donovan

The taxi that came to take me to Sherbrooke Mill was an old, black Mercedes limousine, the kind of vehicle that attracts stares. I sat up front, next to the driver. The transmission was ready to give out and thumped noisily as we swept grandly up the Crumlin Road, the dividing line between hostile Protestant and Catholic sections in West Belfast. That I was an outsider wherever I went was obvious, but I tried to keep a low profile, to be as inconspicuous as possible. It is not possible to arrive anywhere in a black Mercedes limousine and be inconspicuous.

Sherbrooke Mill was once a linen mill, in the days when Ulster was famous all over the world for its linen—before linen was replaced by cotton and cotton was replaced by synthetics, before even synthetic textiles were proved no longer to be a viable industry in Northern Ireland. The looming blackstone buildings sat empty and rotting until a visionary Catholic priest named Joseph Donovan formed a company to buy them up and brought some kind of hope to this area of seedy shops and bombed-out churches.

There's a gate at Sherbrooke Mill with a guard and a tail-wagging "watchdog" watching over a new litter of puppies. On the second floor of one of the buildings Father Donovan, in a turtleneck, cardigan, and loafers, asked permission to light his pipe and showed me a cardboard model of what he's doing with 150,000 square feet of industrial space: dozens of small businesses can set up shop in one area, with an "incubator area" for training people who want to start them; here's the building for YTP classes (I suspect they're not boring and useless here, if Father Donovan has anything to say about it), the restaurant will go in that spot, a theater is under way next to it.

We moved at a trot through the buildings, elevators, stairs, long hallways—through the dream that is becoming reality. From one of the dusty windows on the top floor I could see Samson and Goliath, the giant cranes at the shipyards to the east. On the way back to his office we passed a bronze panel sculptured in low relief: two women intently regard a small, barefoot, weeping child, taken from a painting called *The Lost Child*, by a local artist.

"The child could represent the Catholics of Northern Ireland," he said, "but now, because they're feeling abandoned by the British, that child could represent the Protestants. Or maybe the lost child is Northern Ireland and the two women trying to figure out what in hell to do with it are the governments in England and the Republic."

But Donovan is no lost child himself. He knows exactly where he's going. Fifteen years ago when the stained glass windows of his church farther up the Crumlin Road were blown out by bombs, the government gave him money to replace them. That became the seed money for Sherbrooke Mill. Father Donovan asked for a year off from his duties as parish priest to work on this project. He has been at it for five years now; and he wants to keep going, another five, another ten, whatever it takes to build *hope*. He still says mass every morning at his old church.

"People talk about reconciliation in terms of building bridges. But bridges are to join two equals. What you have in Northern Ireland, Belfast in particular, are one way up here and one way down here. Bridges won't join them. You have to scale a cliff face! Now the Protestants feel very threatened and therefore very defensive, the Catholics feel downtrodden and aggrieved. So you find a way to put them on the same level. The two groups work together here at Sherbrooke. There's only been one ugly incident in five years." He didn't tell me what it was.

Also in his office is a second cardboard model of a shopping-mall complex to go up in the middle of Ardoyne. And in place of the ugly "peace wall" that keeps two warring communities apart, he foresees a row of craft shops. Meanwhile, the church got its stained glass windows several years ago, and he solicits money from the United States. Pictures of the Pittsburgh Steelers hang in the reception area.

Father Donovan is a rare item in Northern Ireland: an optimist. I met hardly anyone in that country who thought things were actually going to improve. Donovan believes it. He even sees the emigration of so many Irish as a positive thing. "This is a very small place, geographically and in other ways. The Irish are dreamers and poets who need space—which is why they thrive in America. And they work so much harder in America than they do at home! Here they would never dream of holding two jobs. They prefer to spend their time in pubs, or watching football. But get the Irish to America—and they end up in the White House!"

St. Peter's High School

I thought I had the bus system figured out; in any case, I didn't want to arrive in the Catholic housing estate in a Mercedes limo. But the bus went only as far as a neighborhood with curbs painted red-white-and-blue, a Protestant area. The Catholic neighborhood was two miles away, according to the bus driver, and up a long hill.

I stopped in a library to use the phone to let the principal know I was going to be late. But the sympathetic librarian heard my problem and offered to take me to the edge of the Catholic area. I would have to go on from there alone, she said.

We drove up the hill and through a Protestant housing estate. The librarian said it had won a prize for being the tidiest area. "It's because there are no shops that it maintains its genteel quality." Some people would call it sterile.

We came to a bump in the road, the kind meant to slow down traffic. This one marked the dividing line between Catholic and Protestant areas. But the librarian, a white-haired lady in her sixties, hesitated only a moment. Then she plucked up her courage and drove on—right to the door of the high school. I believe she did it because she was worried about my safety. When I told the principal, Miss McConville, about my lift, she said, "Most Protestants consider this 'Apache territory.' They think it's very dangerous."

St. Peter's—not its real name—was built in the mid-1970s when thousands of families fled the Falls area of Belfast for safer places away from one of the worst "flash points" of the Troubles. "That was the biggest population shift in the history of Europe," said Miss McConville, a historian. The area around St. Peter's was originally designed for two-family houses, Protestant on one half, Catholic on the other. The planners were certainly not realists, and the scheme did not work; the area is totally Catholic. The planners made another error: the school was built for nine hundred students. Only half that number enrolled.

A small group of boys and girls waited quietly. They wore school uniforms, and when I walked in they stood up one by one and stated their names without being asked. They were in their third year, all about fourteen. Miss McConville appeared with a tea tray, and one of the girls stepped forward and poured me a cup. They eyed the plate of biscuits on the tray, but they wouldn't take any.

These students were polite and reserved, totally unlike the bunch in Ardoyne, but it was no easier to get a conversation going. "It's boring here," they said, sighing and shuffling their feet. "There's nothing to do. The community center closes for the summer when school closes, and even when it's open, it's not that good. They let in kids that are too young."

A tall, thin boy talks of being a professional bicycle racer and belongs to a cycling club. "It it wasn't for that," he said, "there'd be nothing for me."

They've got important exams coming up in a couple of years, but they haven't thought much beyond that. They shrugged off questions about the Troubles. Bombs go off all the time, they said; it means nothing. One boy has been out of the country on a project aimed at breaking down barriers between Catholics and Protestants, but it was a failure from his viewpoint: "The Prod boys wanted to fight us. They sat around doodling Union Jacks just to provoke us."

They thought I'd be interested to know about the Mormon girl in their school: 449 Roman Catholics and one Mormon. I asked them how she got here. "They paid her to change," the students said. "Gave her money to stop being a Catholic and become a Mormon. And she did it. She got special permission so she doesn't have to pray with the rest of us." I didn't believe the part about paying her, but I didn't argue with them.

They weren't comfortable talking politics, but television is the universal language. They watch it all the time, and most of their families seem to own VCRs. Their favorite program is something called "Spitting Image" that uses marionettes to poke fun at political figures like Margaret Thatcher and Ronald Reagan and the Pope. Television has made them experts on crime in America, and they questioned me closely about that. They also wanted to talk about American car manufacturer John DeLorean. His factory built in this area had given work to hundreds of men. When the factory shut down, the men went back on the Bru. The students were curious about DeLorean's drug deals.

Later, in the principal's office, Miss McConville cautioned me about my "Protestant work ethic." I said I thought Catholics must be depressed and suffering from lack of self-esteem as a result of high unemployment which keeps thousands of able-bodied men sitting at home with nothing to do. She said that's Protestant thinking. "Protestants who are out of work will pick up and go somewhere else," she contended. "Catholics stay put. They're more accepting." According to Miss McConville, unemployment doesn't cause depression among Catholics—that's a *Protestant* reaction.

Then she asked me what we talked about in the group. I told her, in vague terms.

"Did you talk about conservation?" she asked.

"No."

She looked deflated. The school has a special kind of garden, a conservation project. The garden was her idea. "The school is very well known for that," she said. But no one had mentioned it.

Deirdre O'Mally

A pretty nineteen-year-old student at Queen's University who worries about her big hips, Deirdre lives in a world far from the boys I had been meeting in high schools and at the youth center. Her background is middle-class, her goals are middle-class. She is studying pharmacy and wants someday to have her own chemist's shop (meaning, drug store). Marriage is something in the distant future, although she has a boyfriend who is a medical student.

"We click," she said. "We have lots of silly fun together,

but I'm not interested in settling down yet. I want to find out who I am, before I'm somebody's missus."

The O'Mallys are a close family. Her father owns a small restaurant that he runs with her older brother, and her mother, whom she describes as a "culchie"—country woman—works three nights a week in a hospital. There are always lots of kids hanging around the house, until her mother gets tired of it and sweeps everyone out for a while. Deirdre says it's important to her to have her father's trust. "If I want to go away on holidays with my boyfriend and Da says, 'I trust you but I'd rather you didn't go,' then I stay home. I'd rather do that than go knowing he doesn't quite approve."

When Deirdre was fifteen, she was chosen by the principal of her convent school to be one of seven girls from that school to go to the United States with Channels of Peace. A group of fifteen-year-olds, evenly divided Protestant and Catholic, male and female, stayed for a month in a small town in Ohio. She jumped at the chance, she said, but peace and reconciliation turned out to be not all peaches and cream.

"It was 2:00 A.M. when we arrived, and there were all the media, television crews, and reporters turning out to meet us. I was appalled at how overbearing Americans can be. We were all exhausted and I was homesick at first, but then I got to be fond of my host family. Amy and I and a boy from Belfast and an American boy got to be a very tight foursome. John, the Belfast boy, became my closest friend. He still is, but for a while we thought we were in love. That was inevitable, I guess, but it didn't really work at all. Now I check out my sweethearts with him, and he does the same with me."

Certain things about her host family bothered her. One was the way they pronounced her name. "They called me DEE-druh," she complained. "Amy, the daughter, was terribly disrespectful to her parents. She whined for whatever she wanted. She expected her mother to chauffeur her around wherever she decided to go, buy her whatever she thought she had to have. I'm not used to that."

Now Deirdre was to be a youth leader for Channels of Peace, going to a different U. S. town this summer. I asked what she thought of it. "The project is looking for future leaders," she said. "It's not supposed to be a way to get slum kids away on holiday. But some of the kids go just for the crack. It's hard to tell what happens when they get back here."

"What do you want for Northern Ireland?"

"In my heart I'm a Republican," she said. "One Irish nation is a romantic ideal, but it's not practical. The South is very poor. The standard of living is much higher here in the North. I wouldn't want to lose those social benefits, not for a romantic notion."

We were sitting in the bar at a hotel where a pianist was playing a medley of Irish songs. Our conversation drifted to a stop while Deirdre listened to her favorite, which seemed to be everybody's favorite at that time. "The Fields of Athenry" is a shamelessly romantic song about a prison ship and a lover sent away from Ireland forever.

II

PROTESTANT BELFAST: WHICH FOOT DO YOU DIG WITH?

My room at Miss Drumm's Guest House was an old-fashioned bedroom with high arched windows looking out on a front garden full of spring flowers. The bathroom, at the back of the house, was shared by a number of guests, American tourists and businessmen from the Republic and the U.K. We nodded politely at breakfast, served in the dining room by Miss Drumm herself, and we worked our way through Northern Ireland's beloved "Ulster Fry"—lean bacon, egg, sausage, grilled tomato, "wheaten bread," piles of butter, jars of marmalade, pots of tea.

Miss Drumm could not pronounce my non-Irish name, adding an *s* and calling me "Miss Meers." She tolerated—barely—the fact that I used her guest house as an office, making strings of telephone calls from the pay phone in the dark hallway, feeding 10-pence pieces into the slot from a hoarded sack. On my first night in Belfast I had stayed in a regular hotel, a room with a bathroom, a telephone, and a television, but it was miles from the center of town, cost more than I could afford, and reeked of Chinese cooking from the restaurant downstairs. The next day I moved to Miss Drumm's on a tree-lined street near Queen's University, a brisk walk from the city center. I liked it there, even without the luxury of a telephone.

Two blocks away was the Wellington Park Hotel, an expensive place hidden behind a high security fence. The hotel had been bombed several times, and the pub next to it, a student hangout called the Bot, completely destroyed. The pub was rebuilt and fills up nightly (except Sundays) with a noisy young crowd. One Sunday night when I was hungry and there were scarcely any restaurants open in Belfast (the whole country comes to a standstill on Sundays), I walked over to the Wellington Park. The guard peered into my purse in an offhand way and waved me through.

The dining room was nearly deserted except for a couple seated at the next table. I treated myself to lamb chops, which turned out to be greasy and tough. The couple nearby seemed to be struggling with their chops, too. We began to talk.

The first question strangers must *always* answer for themselves in Northern Ireland is "Which foot do you dig with?"—meaning, are you Catholic or Protestant? I had heard the expression before and learned the source of it from a sheep farmer in a pub in the Republic who took my little notebook and drew sketches of two different kinds of spades, one traditionally used by Celtic/Irish/Catholic farmers, the other by Scottish/planter/Protestant farmers. Different spades, different feet to dig with, different religions, different cultures. I had been in Northern Ireland long enough to learn how to play the game.

The first "foot" test is names. Catholics usually (but not always) are named for saints—Patrick, Bernadette, Mary, Michael—or have Gaelic (GAY-lik) names—Seamus, Sean,

Eamonn, Maeve, Mairead. Protestants are given names like Trevor, Ernest, Mabel, Ruth, Donald, Muriel. There are, of course, many first names ("Christian names") that are neutral, like Steven, Robert, and Ann. Then you go on to the last name ("surname"), grouping anything with an O' (O'Reilly, O'Shea) and most, but not all, Mc's (McNamara, McHugh) in the Catholic column.

Next, find out where the stranger went to school. Catholics and Protestants attend separate schools, and if there's a saint's name (St. Gabriel's, St. Monica's) or "convent" in the title, it's unquestionably Catholic; if it doesn't *sound* Catholic, it probably isn't—although there are exceptions to that rule, too.

Then the third test is the part of town in which the stranger lives, or where the stranger grew up. The neighborhoods may have been across the street from each other, like the Shankill and the Falls, or on opposite sides of town, but those neighborhoods are exclusively Catholic or Protestant.

There are some people who claim they can tell by *looks* if a person is Catholic or Protestant—how close together the eyes are or the flatness of the face. Another clue is called the "H" Test: Protestants pronounce the letter name "aitch," as Americans do, and Catholics say "haitch." One more: Protestants call the city on the banks of the River Foyle *Londonderry*, but to Catholics it's invariably *Derry*.

A young lawyer entertained me with the story of his lunch with the local cardinal, a top-ranking dignitary of the Catholic church, who went through the usual questions to determine which foot the lawyer dug with. The lawyer took delight in giving the cardinal a hard time. Robert's first name is one that could be either; so is his last name—McAllister. When the cardinal asked where Robert lived, he answered with the name of the local parish church, although the area is mixed. And when the cardinal asked where he had gone to school, Robert threw another curve, mentioning a well-to-do private school where there are at least a few Catholics. I know that

Robert is CofI, because he told me so. He admitted that his game with the cardinal was unfair—"After all, I knew what *he* is"—but Robert enjoyed it anyway.

Donny and Muriel

The couple I met in the hotel dining room were celebrating the eighteen-month "anniversary" of the day they met. They're planning to get married, but they haven't told their families yet. In any case, they will have none of the problems that Ian and Maureen have endured—they're both Protestant. They didn't have to tell me that. If I hadn't been able to figure it out from their names, I would have known by their neighborhoods: he's from the Shankill in West Belfast, and she's from Ballymacarrett in East Belfast, both Protestant areas. There was one more clue: both of them work for the police force. Few Catholics are policemen or work for the RUC which, until recently, has always been regarded as partial to the Protestants.

Donny is a skinny young man with prominent, pale-blue eyes; Muriel has a marvelous mane of dark red hair. She was wearing a light summer dress and white sandals without stockings; I was bundled up as usual in a suit with a sweater and my soggy "rain shoes." We finished our lamb chops, but the conversation kept going despite my problem with their accents. When they talked about the RUC, they lowered their voices; being a policeman, or even a civil servant working for the police, is dangerous business. It is especially dangerous to work at their barracks, a police station in a small, troublesome Catholic section of East Belfast.

Muriel knows from experience how bad it is. Her father had been a police inspector before an IRA bomb blew him away fifteen years ago, when she was eleven. It was almost the first thing she told me about herself.

And Donny said that he was prepared to fight for his country, if it got to that. "I don't want to fight, but if anybody tries to force anything on me. . . ." The thought of it set him scowling.

Force *what* on him?

"If the South, the Republic, really has a say in what's going on here, like the Anglo-Irish agreement says. If the North is ever expected to become part of a united Ireland."

Donny, like most Protestants, is dead set against anything to do with the South, which he sees as backward, completely under the domination of the Catholic Church, the slave of the Pope. He thinks that if Rome were running the country, instead of the British Parliament at Westminster, there would be no divorce, for one thing, and no birth control, and the Catholics who breed like rabbits anyway would multiply and take over everything, driving out people like Donny and Muriel, who are loyal to the Crown and see themselves as British subjects. Donny believes that if the British army were to pull out of Northern Ireland, where they have been keeping the peace—after a fashion—since 1969, there would be civil war, a bloodbath.

Donny doesn't want that, but it's a possibility he thinks he must face. The previous summer he had visited an uncle in Wisconsin and didn't want to come back. But he is an only child, and his mother couldn't stand the idea of his moving away. Muriel has her widowed mother to think about. So they'll stay, although many young people don't hesitate, if they have the opportunity. They leave.

Ernie Phillips

Ernie is a farmer, up from County Down for an agricultural show, and he had offered to help me with names and suggestions. He once studied in Canada and traveled around the U.S. by Greyhound bus. Americans were nice to him, he remembered, and he wanted to return some of that hospitality. He wished, though, that my needs were less difficult. He believes that most Americans sympathize with the Catholics against the Protestants, an unfair attitude he blames on the media, and he was full of warnings. A conservative man in gold-rimmed glasses, he prepared me for suspicion, for reluctance to talk. He told me to "proceed with caution" in most parts of West Belfast, west of the River Foyle in Londonderry, and in the southern part of County Armagh near the border. "Otherwise it's much safer than an American city or Dublin," he said.

Ernie also told me to watch my language. "Referring to locals as 'Irish' and Northern Ireland as 'the North' might raise a few hackles among the majority community," he said. "Protestants don't like to be called 'Irish,' which implies Catholic, and calling this 'the North' makes it sound as though it's part of the South and that the two might someday be united."

"What are you?" I asked him.

"An Ulsterman," he said.

The country that Donny is prepared to defend is less than 5,500 square miles with a population of about a million and a half—a million Protestants and half a million Catholics. Belfast is the capital; its 363,000 people represent about 25 percent of the country's population. Before the partition in 1920, Ireland—the whole island—was divided into four provinces, Ulster, Leinster, Munster, and Connaught, and subdivided into thirty-two counties. At the partition, six of the nine counties of Ulster became Northern Ireland, cutting loose the three counties which had a large Catholic majority. The counties of Northern Ireland are: Down, Armagh (ar-MAH), Fermanagh (fer-MAN-ah), Tyrone, Londonderry, and Antrim. Protestants refer to this as "Ulster," but when a Catholic says "Ulster" the term usually includes those three lost counties, Cavan and Monaghan to the south and Donegal to the west, now part of the Republic.

What both Donny and Ernie fear is loss of power and control—to the Catholics. There are two possible ways of losing power. One, if the British Parliament backs down on its promise to keep the peace and British troops are pulled out; then, many Protestants believe, there would be a civil war. The Catholics of the South would rush to the aid of the Catholics in the North and overwhelm the Protestants, who would be reduced to a minority.

The second way is if the population changes. If Catholics gain in numbers and outvote Protestants, they might elect to withdraw from the United Kingdom and join the South. Such a change is not impossible. Catholic families tend to be large—six, seven, twelve, sixteen children. Most Protestants have only two or three. One of the ways Protestants keep Catholics from catching up in population is to discriminate against them in housing and jobs, forcing them to leave. Most go to England. The trouble is that many Protestants leave too: the job situation is depressing, no matter which foot you dig with.

Many Protestants seem to have a "siege mentality." Although they are a clear majority in Northern Ireland, they *feel* like a threatened minority. Like the whites in South Africa, they are afraid of being overrun by another "tribe" and consumed by another culture.

The Orange Order

To the glorious, pious and immortal memory of King William III, who saved us from Rogues and Roguery, Slaves and Slavery, Knaves and Knavery, Popes

> and Popery, from brass money and wooden shoes; and whoever denies this toast may he be slammed, crammed and jammed into the muzzle of the great gun of Athlone, and the gun fired into the Pope's belly, and the Pope into the Devil's Belly, and the Devil into Hell, and the door locked and the key forever in an Orangeman's pocket.

This is a toast used by the Orange Order, begun somewhere in County Armagh about 1795—a Protestant defense organization, a secret band of night-riding vigilantes. The first members were called the Peep O'Day Boys, who raided Catholic houses at dawn on the excuse of looking for weapons. Two hundred years later the Orange Order is still flourishing. It was named for William of Orange, hero of the Protestants, who defeated Catholic King James II at the Battle of the Boyne in 1690. The Protestants celebrate the event annually on the Twelfth of July with marches through dozens of neighborhoods in Northern Ireland. The marchers wear black bowler hats and orange sashes across their chests, and they step to the boom of the Lambeg drum. (Ironically, the site of the Battle of the Boyne is in the Republic of Ireland, north of Dublin, possibly the last place a loyal Orangeman would go on the Twelfth.)

Boys can join the Orange Order when they're eight years old. There is pressure to join and pressure to stay in the Order or risk being called a "Fenian-lover." (Fenian is a derogatory term for Catholics; another is "taig" or "teague," from *Tadhg*, the Irish version of Timothy and Theodore.) The night before, on the eleventh of July, huge bonfires are lit and anti-Catholic songs fill the air:

My old man's an Orangeman
No Fenian can deny

He loves to wear the Orange sash
On the twelfth day of July
He looks a lovely picture
Marching with the rope
He'd love to march right on to Rome
And hang the fucking Pope.

Here are a few verses of another popular Orange song:

Falls were made for burning
Taigs were made to kill
You've never seen a road
Like the Shankill.
If Taigs were made for killing
Then blood is made to flow
You've never seen a place
Like the Sandy Row.

If guns were made for shooting,
Then skulls are made to crack
You've never seen a better Taig
Than with a bullet in his back.

(Falls, Shankill, and Sandy Row are parts of Belfast.)

"Croppies Lie Down" is an old song that is still sung ("Croppies" refers to Catholics):

Poor Croppies, ye know that your sentence was come,
When you heard the dread sound of the Protestant drum.
In memory of William we hoisted his flag,
And soon the bright Orange put down the Green rag.

The gigantic Lambeg drum, about four feet thick and five feet across, has been called the "ancient Scottish weapon of psychological warfare" because of its roaring boom. It is beaten by bamboo canes tied with leather straps to the drummer's wrists. Throughout the night the drum is beaten, until the wrists have been rubbed raw and bloody. I never heard a Lambeg drum—I was gone before the marching season began—but descriptions I have read of it convinced me that it must indeed be a terrifying sound. It did and does still have its effect on Catholics.

Ian Paisley

The Rev. Dr. Ian R. K. Paisley, M.P., a huge, bellowing preacher with trembling jowls, is one of the best-known Protestants in Northern Ireland, famous for his ranting tirades against the Catholics. About the time I arrived, Paisley and 30,000 of his followers marched through the pretty little town of Hillsborough in County Down where six months earlier Margaret Thatcher, Prime Minister of the U.K., and Garret FitzGerald, Prime Minister in the Republic, had signed the Anglo-Irish agreement, giving the Catholic South a say in Northern affairs. Paisley announced that he and his people had come to "fumigate" the village and to send Parliament a clear message: "Ulster still says no."

Years ago Paisley was thrown in jail for one of his demonstrations, but a three-month imprisonment made him even more popular. His main appeal is to poor Protestants, but he gets his financial support from wealthy Unionists who benefit from keeping Catholics in an inferior position.

Paisley is the son of a Baptist minister who ordained him. Later he got a mail-order diploma in the U.S. and learned his thunderous preaching style at Bob Jones University in Arkansas. In the 1950s he formed his own church, the Free Presbyterians. The massive church he built in Belfast, Mar-

tyrs Memorial Free Presbyterian Church, is the most expensive church erected in the U.K. since World War II. The "M.P." after his name stands for Member of Parliament; he was elected by the ultra-conservative Protestants of his district to represent them in the British Parliament.

I was the *only* female without a hat in the church adrift in a sea of feathers, veils, and draped chiffon. Outside, electronic bells banged out hymns, and people hurried toward the big front door. A fleet of eight buses was parked in the lot behind the church. The church seats maybe a thousand people. Men at the front door shook hands with everyone, looked me in the eye, and asked me where I was from. It was a kind of security check.

An enormous pulpit with three microphones dominates the front of the church, but the booming voice of Mr. Paisley certainly did not require them. He wore a black frock coat and looked and sounded like a Puritan minister in seventeenth century New England. After some hymns and psalms, Paisley preached with considerably less of the fire-and-brimstone than I had been led to expect, and none of the scathing attacks on Catholics for which he is infamous. His prayers were more interesting, not so much *asking* God as *telling* Him. The Almighty was instructed, in no uncertain terms, to destroy the Anglo-Irish agreement.

James Reid, Kirkwood College

"The tragedy," said the headmaster, "is that the best and brightest are gone. One way or another, they all leave."

We were standing in the hush of the Great Hall of Kirkwood College with its hundreds of school portraits of eager graduates who had been killed in the two world wars. Most of the rest—the talented, ambitious, well-educated ones—

had left for other shores and never come back. One of the major problems of Ireland, both North and South, is the Brain Drain. Most people say there is no future for such bright young men here, and off they go. I heard this refrain over and over: all the best leave. So do many of the second best. They believe they have no choice.

But some do come back. James Reid is one who did.

Reid is an elegant man, the head of an elegant school, one of several in Northern Ireland that cater to educating the "cream of the crop" (or, in the view of some cynics, the "thick and rich"). We had been sitting in deep leather chairs in Reid's office with a portrait of Winston Churchill and a stuffed boar's head peering down at us. The green lawn, old trees, and blossoming shrubbery beyond the windows reminded me of an English country estate, although the school is only a few miles east of the shipyards on Belfast Lough (a lough, pronounced LOKH, is an arm of the sea or a large lake).

Reid's Protestant parents were from the South, where they were discriminated against because of their religion ("I know what discrimination is all about"), so his father, a doctor, moved the family to Malaysia. Reid was born in Singapore, where his father was imprisoned by the Japanese during World War II. After the war the family returned to Ireland, but this time to the North. James grew up in County Down and was educated at Cambridge, England. After teaching for ten years in the U.K., he came to Kirkwood College in 1976. One of his goals was to merge Kirkwood with a nearby girls' school, but the "Old Kirkwoodians" would not hear of such a break with tradition. The school remains a steadfastly male—and Protestant—stronghold.

Reid drifted into the subject of politics. "I deplore the local politicians," he said, "but it's hard to get a good one to run for office. People are not willing to take the time needed for basic changes, and so they throw out their officials every couple of years and elect equally ineffectual new ones. I'd love to be Prime Minister for ten years without having to run for office. Then it would be possible to make changes." He didn't say what the changes might be.

The main building is a huge Victorian brick pile with looming turrets and gloomy oak paneling. The college was founded in 1894 by a man who left a hundred acres to provide a "liberal, Protestant education." Before the Troubles, boys from well-to-do families from all over the British Empire traveled to Kirkwood College for their education. No longer; most students who want to go abroad for their schooling go to Canada or the U.K. instead.

Three quarters of the students are admitted on the basis of merit, their scores on tests administered to all schoolchildren in Northern Ireland; another quarter buy their way in, regardless of their test scores; these are the "thick and rich."

"One of the things I'd like to be able to do," Reid said, "is to admit children who don't make the grades that will entitle them to a free education." A third are boarding students from outside Belfast or from other parts of the U.K.; the rest are day students. A handful are Catholics.

Most of the graduates continue their studies at universities. Many go to Queen's University in Belfast, but the more adventurous strike out for institutions "across the water," a Belfast term that means east to Great Britain, not west to Canada or the United States.

When the rain let up we went outside, past the small lake, the more recently built dormitories, the innumerable rugby and cricket fields, and the oval where a lone runner skimmed solitary hurdles on the muddy track. Nearly all the students had already gone for the weekend. Through the trees, there were glimpses of the gleaming white buildings of Stormont, where the government of Northern Ireland has its offices.

"Things don't blow up when everything is in turmoil,"

the headmaster said as we started back. "It's when things are quiet that they're most likely to explode. And letting off steam gradually doesn't work either. Look what's happening to South Africa. It's just when you think you've lowered the pressure that the whole thing goes berserk."

Samson and Goliath

Two gigantic cranes, nicknamed "Samson" and "Goliath," stand like sentries at Harland and Wolff shipyards, where the River Lagan flows into Belfast Lough. With their twin monograms, H & W, they are a dramatic part of the cityscape visible from most parts of Belfast, but they disappear as you get close, after passing endless blocks of factory buildings and two checkpoints. The cranes are powerful symbols in Belfast.

They are symbols of a lost prosperity. Harland and Wolff was founded in 1858, although the history of shipbuilding in this part of Ireland began a couple of centuries earlier. The company did well for itself; in 1911 a ship called the *Olympic,* 46,000 tons and 860 feet long, slid down the ways, followed a year later by an even larger sister ship named the *Titanic.* On its maiden voyage on April 15, 1912, the *Titanic* hit an iceberg in mid-Atlantic and sank. More than 1,500 people died in the disaster.

When World War I broke out, Harland and Wolff shifted into high gear to build warships. In World War II the shipyard produced 139 naval vessels, even though German air attacks wiped out about 60 percent of the facility in the spring of 1941. Within two years most of the shops were in production again. That was the company's heyday—23,000 men worked for H & W.

Since then there has been a sharp decline, partly because

of decreased demand and partly because of mechanization. Today Harland and Wolff employs only about 5,000 men. Nearly all of them are Protestant. For Catholics who can't get jobs at H & W, Samson and Goliath are symbols of blatant discrimination.

James Reid had mentioned people he knows who work quietly for reconciliation between Catholics and Protestants. "That's one of the stories behind the headlines," he said. "Obviously there are tremendously dedicated adults and some idealistic young people trying hard—and probably an equal number of cynics who wonder what good it's doing."

One evening I talked with one of those idealistic young people. Peter Downey is a schoolteacher involved in various programs to get underprivileged children out of Belfast on holiday. This is in addition to his classes at a primary school, and his work on the school play which had been in production since last fall. Peter sings in the church choir. He's a youth leader. He has been to America with Channels of Peace. He's in his twenties, blond, blue-eyed, handsome, and very serious.

We felt pretty comfortable with each other, so I asked him about the discrimination in hiring I had heard many Catholics complain about—like at Harland and Wolff.

Peter was instantly tense and on the defensive. "It's not prejudice, it's custom," he said. "Catholics don't live near the shipyards, so they don't work there. It's not that they are refused jobs—they don't want them. They'd rather work for companies in their own neighborhoods."

I didn't argue, but he must have seen the doubt written all over my face, a look that said, "It can't be that simple." It was easier to talk about other things.

After a while he grinned a little sheepishly and said, "I got pretty defensive, didn't I?"

"You did."

"I guess everybody is prejudiced, at least a little. We all see things from our own perspective. You probably do, too."

Of course I do. I admitted a natural bias toward the underdog, the one out of power.

"You mean the Catholics."

"Yes."

That confession made him wonder if I could back off and be totally objective, letting each side speak for itself. I wondered that, too.

"The problem here is, nobody knows anything firsthand," Peter said. "We only know it secondhand, or even more remote than that."

The challenge then, it seemed to me, was to find out things firsthand. And one way to do that was to visit Harland and Wolff.

T. John Palmer has the status of folk hero in Northern Ireland. Palmer started with H & W in the 1950s, worked his way up to top-level management, and went to England for a few years. Normally that would have been the last of him, but Palmer did an un-Irish thing: *he came back*. Now he is head of Harland and Wolff, which even with its work force reduced to a fraction of its former strength is still one of Northern Ireland's biggest employers.

I didn't try to see Palmer, although that would have been interesting. I wanted to talk with someone involved with young people and managed to set up an appointment with a man I'll call Mr. Woods. With gray hair combed smoothly back, a trendy striped shirt, dark-rimmed glasses that he uses for reading and punctuation, and an annoying habit of jabbing my arm with his elbow to make sure I got his point, Mr. Woods really didn't want to be talking to me. He kept trying to figure out who had given me his name. It was the switchboard operator.

There were no regular tours of the shipyard, but I asked Mr. Woods to show me around the Training Center, where apprentices are taught the various crafts of shipbuilding—pipe fitting, electrical work, welding. The apprentice program could accommodate two hundred boys, but because of the depressed economy in the country in general and in the shipbuilding industry in particular, they take on only fifty. There are six hundred applicants for those fifty places, thirty boys competing for every opening.

I asked how the fifty are picked. Mr. Woods mentioned the ninety-minute battery of tests that cover a variety of skills. About half the applicants wash out as a result of the tests; the rest are called in for interviews. The director of the program makes the decision blindly without ever meeting the boys himself, relying on reports of the interviewers so that the decision is "totally unbiased."

We had wandered through the battleship-gray hallways past models of Harland and Wolff ships and talked about Mr. Woods's own history with the company. He collected a packet of materials for me, a history of the company, a glossy brochure about the kinds of work being done now, the sorts of vessels under development. Mr. Woods wondered if I had any more questions. It was hot in his office, I really couldn't think of anything polite to ask, so I decided to take a risk.

"I know it's a question you don't like to be asked," I began gingerly, "but what about the claim that this is a totally Protestant company and that Catholics can't get jobs here?"

The change was amazing. Woods spread his feet and hauled up his trousers by the belt like a boxer climbing into the ring. He moved closer, literally backing me against a filing cabinet, and launched into a tirade.

He has a Catholic secretary, he said, jabbing me with his elbow. Two girls in personnel are Catholics, jab. A few of the boys in the apprentice program are Catholic, jab. He's on the board of governors of two Catholic schools, jab jab. *It is never a factor*! Why, you're not allowed to ask an applicant's religion on the form. (But you are allowed to ask his name, his address, and the school he attended; you don't *need* to ask his religion. I didn't mention that.)

He fumbled among stacks of papers and produced a forty-year-old photograph, taken on the occasion of the retirement of a company official. The picture was taken before Woods even joined the organization, but he recognized most of the sixty-some men seated formally in long rows. "*This* man is Catholic . . . *this* man is Catholic . . . *this* man is Catholic . . ." He located a half dozen.

It's a matter of geography, he insisted; they won't travel over to Queen's Island, to the shipyards, from west, north, or south Belfast, where they all live.

Then he launched into the story of the two RC lads in the program who had been issued coveralls, lockers, passcards—everything they needed to work—but when the career counselor from their school came to visit, they were gone, their coveralls and passcards neatly stacked in their empty lockers. So there you are! Once the principal of one of the Catholic schools asked him, "Why aren't any boys from my school working for you?" And Mr. Woods could name, without even checking his records, three boys—one of whom had been sacked—all from that principal's school.

Woods had story after story to prove his point. I tried to calm him down. "I guess what I'm saying is, I think it's interesting that you can name the Catholics in a forty-year-old photograph, that it's such an issue." That didn't help matters.

It was clearly time for me to get out of there. Mr. Woods called a taxi for me and held the door. We were still smiling politely, somehow. "Call if you have any more questions," he managed to say.

Later I described the scene to my friend Seamus McHugh. "Catholics are scared to death to work at the shipyards," he said, "even if they do manage to get hired. Their fathers were scared, too. And for good reason. When there was trouble, they were the ones who got it. It would be hard to change that."

Trevor Hand

Trevor described himself as a "shy Protestant boy who doesn't give a flip which foot somebody digs with," and I liked him immediately, for those reasons and because he approaches his work the way I do mine, with total immersion. Trevor is a journalist deeply involved in social issues that take him around his country doing in-depth interviews on such subjects as alcoholism, aging, mental illness, homosexuality, subjects that all but the most stout-hearted avoid. Trevor does not.

The shy Protestant boy is in his late twenties, wears jeans, a rumpled tweed jacket, a skinny tie, glasses and shaggy hair—definitely not the blow-dried media type. We met in a museum tea shop one morning; he had brought with him a list of people and organizations he thought I might find interesting. We talked about several taboo subjects, like suicide. If you believe what you read, nobody commits suicide in Ireland, north or south; there is strong religious opposition to it, and sympathetic doctors therefore almost always ascribe death to accidental causes. I remembered a tiny news item I had just seen in the Belfast paper: a high official of the RUC had been found dead in bed with a bullet in his heart. "There is no suspicion of murder," the article said. But the word *suicide* was not mentioned.

Trevor had once interviewed a gay man in a country village

who masked his sexual orientation with heavy drinking. Homosexuality is deplored and gay men are despised in Northern Ireland, but being a drunk is acceptable in male society. Trevor talked with the wives of a couple of alcoholics when he did a series on alcoholism, a major problem in all age groups.

"I asked them if they were embarrassed by their husbands' behavior. What I really was building up to was, 'Do you love him?' "

"What was the answer?"

Both said they were embarrassed.

"One said she didn't love her husband, the other said she loved him anyway. I didn't believe the second one for a moment. [Being alcoholic may be all right among the men, but it's very tough on the wives and families.] I turned off the tape recorder and told her she wasn't being honest."

But my mission was not to focus on suicides, gays, and wives of alcoholics. What Trevor had in mind for me was to track down some of the "uniformed, volunteer youth organizations," like the BB's, the GB's, the GG's, and the Scouts. The Scouts, of course, are the Boy Scouts, founded by Robert Baden-Powell in Great Britain in 1908. The GG's—Girl Guides—are the equivalent of the Girl Scouts. Boys' Brigade and Girls' Brigade, strong throughout the United Kingdom, were founded by William Alexander Smith, an early cohort of Baden-Powell who disagreed with him over the development of the organization. Baden-Powell wanted the emphasis on outdoor life, Smith on spiritual life, and the two went their separate ways.

The Guides and Scouts function mostly through Protestant schools and churches; Catholic clergy thought meeting with Protestants was an "occasion of sin" and formed their own troops. I visited the headquarters of some of the organizations and came away with armloads of brochures showing the glowing faces of earnest young people in dress uniforms arrayed with badges. And then I was invited to a meeting.

Madeline

"Thunder, thunder, thunderation," the leader sang enthusiastically, and some of the Guides joined in. I was hovering at the edge of the annual joint meeting of two troops, one from a prestigious girls' school and one from a special school for the handicapped. The meeting was less than a success.

The groups had gotten together in Northern Ireland's best and newest school for the physically handicapped; the age range is from two-and-a-half to twenty, and mental ability goes from severely retarded but educable all the way to gifted. Most of the children are brought here daily by bus, but some of them stay in residential "chalets." Most of the Girl Guides are residents, teenagers who have spent a big part of their lives here.

The school has a specially equipped greenhouse and kitchen, an art studio and music rooms, and an electronic facility where children with only the smallest range of motion can learn to type. The big, glass-enclosed swimming pool on the ground floor was where the joint "meeting" began—about twenty healthy visitors leaping around in the water like well-fed seals and a dozen or so girls in wheelchairs behind a safety wall, watching the fun.

"I can't go swimming. I take fits," said a girl with huge blue eyes and LORRAINE stenciled on the back of her wheelchair. She introduced a tall, pretty girl named Michelle who is mentally retarded, and Alice, with a bright smile and tiny stumps for legs. An outspoken girl named Diane said she was looking forward to a weekend home in Enniskillen, far from Belfast. "I've been here too long," Diane said.

Madeline, who had achieved ranger status and is an assistant to the adult leaders of the visiting group, sat with us behind the wall. She wore a Guide uniform and seemed very sure of herself. Suddenly Madeline began to talk. "A year ago I was extremely shy," she said. "I was so busy studying for my exams I didn't take time for anything else. Now I'm lower sixth [high school junior] and the pressure is off. Of course it will all start again next year. Everything about me changed this year, beginning with getting my hair cut." Her straight brown hair swung at chin-length. "Then I joined a Venture group with boys, which was quite a step, because I've only ever gone to school with girls and I had no *idea* what boys are like."

"I have a wee pump in my brain," Lorraine interrupted. "To stop the fits."

"To show you how much I've changed," Madeline went on, "a friend of mine was having a birthday, and I put on a miniskirt cut up to *here* and fishnet stockings, and I sprayed my hair green and gelled it into spikes. He was properly shocked, I can tell you."

Madeline talked with her hands, toying with her hair. The girls in the wheelchairs watched, taking this in. "I can't wait to get away from here," Diane said.

"I've got this wonderful hat," Madeline said. "I decorate it with hearts, bunnies, shamrocks, depending on the season, you know. It's a very sociable hat. Everyone wants to wear it, and it gets passed around. That hat has been *every*where. Even in the gents' loo!" She giggled. "I'm a totally different person than I was last year. Everything changed."

Hard to imagine how this must have sounded, this free, frivolous life, to girls who go nowhere, attend no parties in miniskirts and fishnet stockings, have no boys to amuse with a sociable hat.

The visiting Guides climbed out of the pool, and we headed toward the art studio for refreshments. "Let me show you how I can race this thing!" Diane called and freewheeled down a ramp, deftly stopping her wheelchair short before it collided with the wall.

The hostess Guides passed out cans of Coke and Fanta and bags of "crisps" (potato chips) to visitors clustered around a table at one side of the room. The hostesses stayed on the other. When "Thunder Thunder Thunderation" petered out, Miss Crossen, the leader, motioned me to a corner of the studio. When she was certain that a pale, fragile girl with pearl earrings would not see her, she pulled out a portfolio of the girl's drawings and watercolors. "Jessica is the most talented student I've had in years," said the leader, who is also the art teacher. "But she gets terribly upset when I show her work to anyone."

Everybody agreed that it was a fine idea to have the visitors come back, once a term. "It's good for your girls to meet girls like this," the leader said. I was thinking that they didn't really *meet*; they needed to find something to do together. There was no tactful way to suggest this. Miss Crossen said, "I won't be here when you come back. I'm quitting. Teaching these girls is a tough job. I'm completely burned out."

I understood how that would happen. But it was one place where the subject of Protestants and Catholics, and who digs with which foot, never came up.

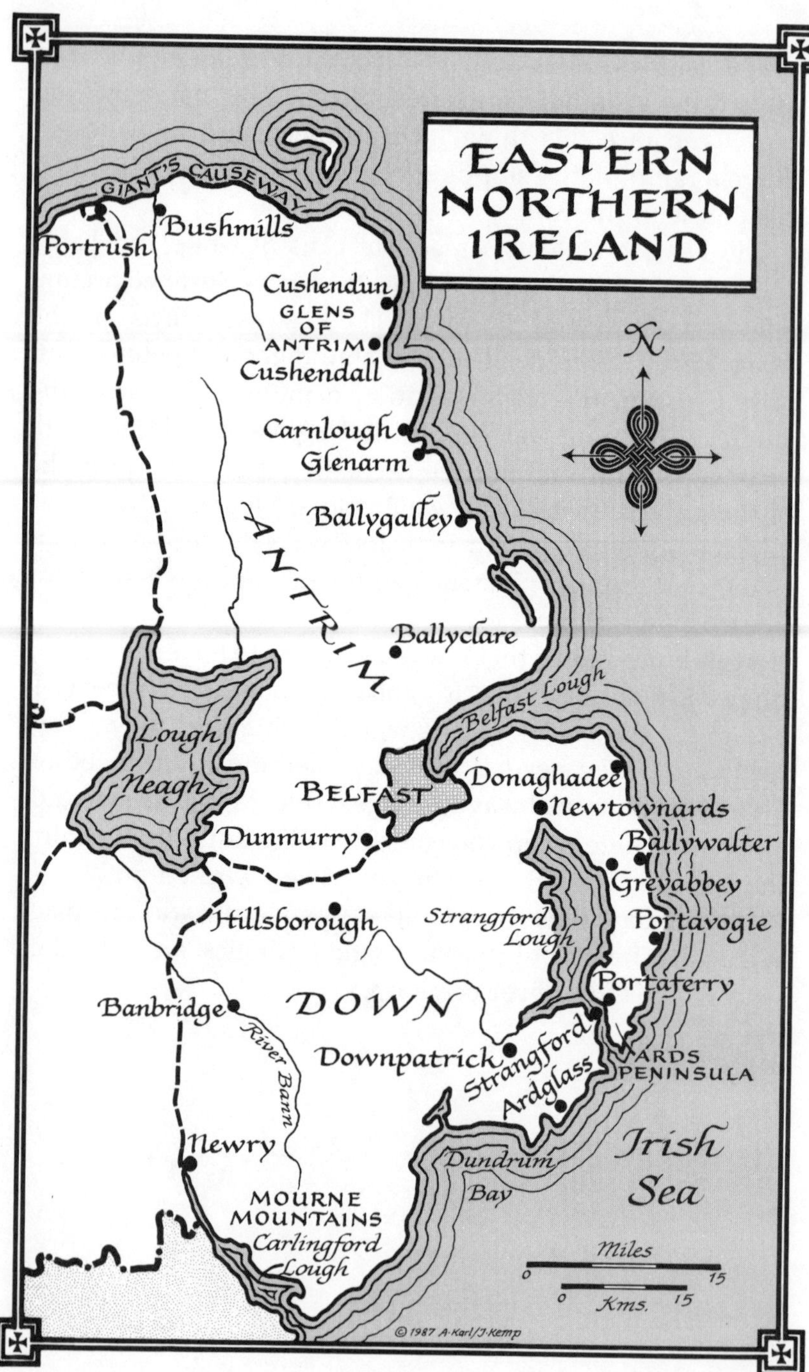
EASTERN NORTHERN IRELAND
N
GIANT'S CAUSEWAY
Portrush
Bushmills
Cushendun
GLENS OF ANTRIM
Cushendall
Carnlough
Glenarm
Ballygalley
ANTRIM
Ballyclare
Belfast Lough
Lough Neagh
BELFAST
Donaghadee
Newtownards
Ballywalter
Greyabbey
Dunmurry
Hillsborough
Strangford Lough
Portavogie
Portaferry
Banbridge
DOWN
Downpatrick
Strangford
Ardglass
ARDS PENINSULA
River Bann
Newry
Irish Sea
Dundrum Bay
MOURNE MOUNTAINS
Carlingford Lough
Miles
0
15
0
Kms.
15
© 1987 A·Karl/J·Kemp

III

COUNTY DOWN: SAINTS, KINGS, AND ORDINARY PEOPLE

Bridie's People

"Come along with us, Caroline," Bridie sang over the telephone. (People invariably pronounced my name with a long *i*, rather than as it's spelled.) "It's an anniversary mass for me late father. You'll meet some of me brothers and their wives."

Seamus came on the line. "It's not as bad as it sounds," he said. "After mass we'll all go back to Bridie's brother's house. It'll be a good crack. You'll see."

So I put on my serious suit and went along with them to Banbridge, a half hour or so southwest of Belfast. "Built by the River Bann, you see," Bridie explained from the backseat. She was not a backseat driver so much as a backseat lecturer, and the trip in the rain—of course it was raining—was filled with bits and pieces of information, much of it family history.

Bridie is the youngest in a family of seven, the only daughter, a position she claims taught her how to handle men.

(Seamus said nothing, glanced at me poker-faced, waggled his eyebrow.) Two brothers live in Banbridge, one a teacher, the other a chemist (druggist) with his own shop. One brother had been a priest but left the priesthood, moved to the United States and married, and now has a child. The other brothers, whom she describes as "arch-conservative Catholics," were hurt by that.

After mass we all trooped over to the chemist's modern house, for refreshments. The custom, I learned, was to have one alcoholic drink, followed by tea. The chemist's wife and daughter wheeled in a trolley loaded with food: cheese and crackers, chocolate cake, apple meringue, sponge cakes with jam centers, and a gigantic teapot. While we ate and drank, snapshots were passed around from the April wedding of a nephew. And thereby a family scandal was revealed.

The bridegroom's father, a smiling gray-haired man, appeared in one photograph with a smiling young wife, quite pregnant. This brother, I learned later, divorced his first wife a few years ago, moved to the Republic, and remarried. Now the father of the bridegroom, he was about to become a father again. The former wife appeared in other snapshots. No one mentioned this while we passed around the photographs, but I filed it away to ask Bridie about later.

Bridie had already told me that she strongly favors birth control, thinks divorce is a legal and personal right, and supports an integrated school system. You could hardly describe Bridie as a fallen-away Catholic; she attends mass daily. But her views are decidedly liberal. The church would call them heretical.

Her brothers' views are not. Liam, the teacher, she described as both rigidly Irish and rigidly Catholic. Liam's philosophy is, if it isn't Irish, it isn't any good. He has given each of his seven children a Gaelic name and insisted that they learn to speak Irish. At the appropriate age, each child was sent off to summer camp in an area called the Gaeltacht in the western part of Ireland where the ancient language is still spoken. There they learned the old songs and the old dances, played sports like Gaelic football, hurling and camogie (the women's version of hurling, a sport played with long sticks and a leather ball), immersed themselves in Irish history and Irish culture, and spoke exclusively Irish—or were sent home.

Sean, the chemist, is not so obsessed with his Irishness. That, according to Bridie, is because his wife is from somewhere around Dublin, and "her ways are more English." It's a narrow view, Bridie claims, that limits the world to Irishness. Catholics in the North who persist in that narrow Irishness, spending summers in the Gaeltacht and so on, place themselves at a further disadvantage when it comes to getting jobs and getting ahead in Northern Ireland.

We were joined by Sean's son Anthony and his girlfriend Cecilia, who had both just finished their exams at Queen's. They were in a jubilant mood—Cecilia had found a job teaching in Newry, a border town, starting in the fall, and Anthony had just learned he had been accepted for a job with an international computer corporation in Dublin. When Anthony's parents weren't listening, Cecilia gleefully described to Uncle Seamus and Aunt Bridie—and me—their weekend in Dublin when Anthony drove down for his interview, a weekend that involved smuggling Cecilia into Anthony's expensive hotel room, paid for by the company.

"When are you getting married?" Aunt Bridie inquired.

"Not until I've taught for a while in Newry," Cecilia said firmly. "I didn't spend all those years at the university just to follow Anthony to Dublin."

Several mentions were made of leaving, but nobody moved. More time passed, and more conversation. It was after eleven when Seamus and Bridie decided, finally, that it was "time to go spit on our own grate," and we were on the road back to Belfast.

Spin backward to a time some twelve thousand years ago when there was no sign of human life in Ireland. In that eon Ireland was still connected to the larger island of Great Britain by a land bridge, and both were still a part of the continent of Europe. The first early humans had reached Britain about 7500 B.C.; it took them another fifteen hundred years to get to Ireland. And so it was about 6000 B.C. when Stone Age people roamed Ireland, a small, dark race known in Irish mythology as the Firbolg. Over the next four thousand years these wanderers settled down, became farmers, and developed bronze tools.

But they were no match for the Celts, Iron Age people who came from Britain a few centuries later. Regarded by Irish nationalists as the "true Irish," these Celtic tribes had moved back and forth all over Europe, reached Britain, and pushed on to Ireland about 350 B.C.

The Celts were a highly advanced pagan society who brought with them a system of law and government and a distinctive language. They divided up the land among clans ruled by chieftains and built their homes in fortified villages. Their language was Gaelic, an ancient tongue distantly related to Latin, Greek, Sanskrit, and other Indo-European languages. Irish colonists carried that language to Scotland, Wales, and the Isle of Man.

The word *Gaelic* was actually an uncomplimentary name given by the Welsh to Irish settlers who came there. But in Ireland *Gael* was used to indicate people who stuck to the native culture and language, in contrast with *Gall,* which referred to the waves of Scandinavian, Norman, and English invaders. Because the word *Gaelic* eventually came to mean so many different things, the historical language of Ireland is now simply called Irish.

One of the challenges of turning a spoken language into a written one is to devise an alphabet. This job fell to early scholars in Ireland, Christian priests who had brought the Latin alphabet with them. Irish uses only eighteen letters to signify more than sixty distinct sounds found in the language. These letters often do not correspond to English sounds, and I discovered that I could not attempt to pronounce most words and proper names from their spellings. I saw the word *failte,* "welcome," many times, but did not guess that it is pronounced FELL-cheh. Nor could I have figured out that Siobhan, the Irish form of Joan, is pronounced sheh-VAHN, or that Sean, meaning John, is pronounced SHAWN. I sympathized with Irish kids shipped off to summer camp in the Gaeltacht where they had to learn to speak this difficult language or suffer immediate banishment.

Seamus's People

We left Belfast in the rain early one Saturday morning, bound for Ardglass, a small fishing village on the east coast. In 1975 when the Troubles were at their height, Seamus's brother Frank took his wife, Rita, and their young children and moved away from their old neighborhood in Belfast to this spot overlooking the sea and the harbor where the fishing boats tie up. Frank's son Joe was twelve at the time, and Frank was afraid the boy would get mixed up in the violence if they stayed in Belfast.

They bought an old stone house in the middle of a weed-grown field next to the ruins of an ancient castle, and they knocked out walls, installed a modern kitchen, pulled weeds, and planted grass. The family adjusted well to life in the country, although the thirty-mile commute to Belfast every day is wearying. Rita opened a little wool shop next to the house. Mary, the oldest girl, works in Belfast, near Frank's office, and rides with him. Kathleen, fifteen, is still in school, and Emma, the youngest, is just "coming eight." Only Joe, now twenty-three, has problems; he lost his job last winter, and prospects for finding another are dim.

The family was gathering in Ardglass for Emma's first communion, and I was invited to go along. On the way we stopped in Downpatrick, the burial place of three beloved saints of Ireland—Patrick, Columba, and Bridget—to buy a special gift. Seamus parked on the main street in the shopping district, and while Bridie went to buy Emma a bracelet and I looked for a bookstore, he stayed in the car. This was necessary because the main street of Downpatrick is a "control area," meaning that cars can't be left unattended—an empty car may be booby-trapped with a bomb. Downpatrick has had its share of bombings, as well as its share of saints.

The children crowded the front pews of the church, girls in long white dresses and veils like miniature brides, boys in handsome white Irish fisherman's sweaters. They sang, recited prayers, read scripture, and sat quietly through the sermon and the mass. The priest offered prayers thanking God for the children and for their parents. We craned our necks for a glimpse of Emma.

The wind was whipping in off the Irish Sea, and families dressed in summer clothes gathered bravely on the lawn outside the church for pictures. Emma was with her parents: her father, Frank, is white haired like Seamus; you could spot him at a considerable distance by his brilliant red necktie ("Has to do with taste, not politics," his wife Rita said). Rita is a tall, handsome woman with masses of dark hair piled on top of her head. Joe, a quiet young man, was there with his equally quiet girlfriend, Rose. Mary, a younger edition of her mother in looks and personality, sparked the conversation, evading direct and indirect questions about exactly where she was the night before until three o'clock in the morning. She hugged herself in the cold wind. Kathleen, dressed up in white polka dots and navy blue stockings, smiled shyly. In front of them stood Emma, the russet-haired and freckled baby of the family. "Our Emma," they call her.

This was a grand occasion, and it was clear that money had been spent generously, not only on the laces and ribbons on the long white dresses and veils but on the accessories: white gloves, white shoes and socks, and one child carried a white parasol trimmed in lace to match her dress. "I don't believe in such show," Rita whispered. "We borrowed Emma's dress from a friend."

It didn't seem to matter to Emma that the dress was a hand-me-down; she was the center of the family's attention. "Isn't she the gorgeous girl, now!" her Aunt Bridie raved.

When the pictures had been taken, everyone ran shivering to the parish hall for tea and biscuits and a chance to shake hands and say a few words to the hearty priest, Father Dominic, who told a joke—about the widow who had her husband's body cremated and put his ashes in an egg timer. Said the widow, "He worked not a day in his life, so he didn't, but he's going to work now, so he is."

We piled into cars and drove miles to a restaurant in Strangford, a pretty town by Strangford Lough. "It's Emma's day," her beaming father said, as he placed her at the head of the table. The restaurant was jammed with celebrating families from Ardglass who had to come all this way because restaurants closer to home were fully booked. Babies howled, brothers and sisters raced noisily between the tables, and girls and boys in their first communion finery tried to remember to behave. Parents ordered wine to drink with their fried fish and chips, and everyone ate warm apple tart piled with fresh whipped cream.

But the day was not over. Back to Ardglass we went, to sit drowsily around the electric fire, digest the big meal, and try to think of ways to amuse ourselves. Emma changed from her white dress into a pink party dress, and her mother tied a matching ribbon in the little girl's long hair. Emma had opened her gifts—Aunt Bridie's bracelet, a red purse containing quite a lot of money, a couple of rosaries, a white missal, a tiny fake camera that showed holy pictures in the viewfinder when you clicked the shutter, and paperback books by American authors Laura Ingalls Wilder and Judy Blume.

Seamus and Bridie love an excuse for silliness, and Seamus began an add-on story about a "sausage dog" named Johann Sebastian Bach. We went around the room, piling one absurdity on top of another. Joe and Rose slipped silently away. Frank fell asleep, snoring gently. The game went on and on.

Kathleen is a talented pianist, but a shy one and could not be persuaded to play. Aunt Bridie needed no coaxing, though, and Rita has a wonderful voice. She shut her eyes and began to sing old Irish ballads with the rest of us joining in the refrain after each of the numerous verses. Rita used to perform in musicals, "But no more—I didn't want to become one of those fat old ladies with a cracking voice still singing about being 'a pretty little maiden,' " she said. So she sticks to the church choir.

The scene reminded Seamus of the time they were sitting around like this and Bridie was picking out a few old tunes, and Rita was singing with everybody joining in. An American tourist came to the door and asked permission to photograph the ruins of the castle next door. He heard the singing, and they invited him in, and the tourist was in tears, actual tears, at finding himself in the midst of such an authentic old-fashioned Irish family.

"A great joke," Seamus said, "because we never sit around and sing like this."

"Except when there's an American in the neighborhood," Bridie said. "They're easily impressed."

* * *

It was late again when we left to "spit in our own grate," driving back through Downpatrick. You can find Patrick's burial place, but you can't find his birthplace in Ireland, because this famous Irish saint was born in Britain. His parents were Roman citizens and Christians. The few available facts about him have been misted over by legend, but it is thought that he was born about A.D. 385. When he was sixteen he was captured by Irish Celts, who took him off to Ireland as a slave. For six years he worked as a shepherd on the northern coast of Ireland. A voice inspired him to escape, and he made his way to Gaul, the ancient name for France, and wandered the continent for a while, eventually ending up a monk in a French monastery. Back to Britain he went, where a vision instructed him to return to Ireland. It took years to accomplish this, but in A.D. 432 he was again on Irish soil, successfully challenging the pagan priests and gaining converts for Christianity.

With the approval of Pope Leo I, Patrick established his official seat in the town of Armagh, perhaps forty miles west of Downpatrick. By the time he died in 461, almost all of Ireland had been Christianized. Patrick was one of the most successful missionaries in history. His personality has been described as "winning," but he was also shrewd. He understood the Celtic temperament, and he knew how to work within the tribal system. Until the English government had it destroyed in 1539, his burial place in Downpatrick was a great European shrine.

Unfortunately Patrick's influence did not last, and soon after his death the Gaels gradually reverted to their old pagan ways, practicing their own Gaelic version of Christianity. By the year 1100 Irish Catholicism was quite different from the Roman Catholicism practiced in most other countries. But Patrick is far from forgotten. March 17, St. Patrick's Day, is still a celebration in Ireland—but perhaps not on the scale it is in America. New Yorkers, who all become Irish for that one day, far outdo anything the Irish of Ireland come up with. Even in Albuquerque, New Mexico, hundreds flock to eat the corned beef and cabbage dinner prepared by the mostly Hispanic members of a large Roman Catholic parish.

Another Downpatrick saint, Columba, was the first great Irish scholar and patron of poets, and his influence too was widely felt in Europe. Also called Colmcille, he was born in 521 in County Donegal. He founded several monastery schools, and he and several other monks sailed to Scotland to Christianize the Scots. Before Columba died in 597, Northern Scotland had become entirely Christian. St. Bridget, the third saint buried here, was born about 453 and died seventy years later, founded a monastery, and is the inspiration for all the girls named Bridget, Brigid, and Bridie.

The overlapping lifetimes of these three saints initiated a golden age of learning in Ireland. For several centuries there were no invasions of the island, and there was time and leisure for scholarship. At this time the Roman Empire had been overrun by barbarians, and Europe was sinking into the Dark Ages. But in Ireland the lamp stayed lit, and eventually culture throughout Europe was rekindled from its flame.

Peace did not endure. Late in the eighth century Vikings began making quick raids in their longboats. Over the next two hundred years they penetrated deeper inland, and some stayed on to build trading towns like Dublin, Waterford, and Cork. The monasteries were the worst hit; they were poorly defended, and the invaders knew they were a good source of provisions.

Warfare at the close of the tenth century was constant, but out of the conflict emerged a hero named Brian Boru, who became the High King of Ireland. Brian managed to unify the country, but not to end the wars. In 1014 an epic battle took place and Brian was killed, but eventually the Vikings were defeated and their influence ended—except for the red hair, typical of the Norsemen. Brian's legendary harp is a symbol throughout Ireland.

Next came the English. Adrian IV, an English pope, was concerned that the Christian religion in Ireland was different from that of Catholics in other parts of Europe. Pope Adrian gave Henry II, an English king, his blessing to invade Ireland and take it as part of his crown inheritance. Henry sent a Welshman nicknamed "Strongbow" to lead the invasion in 1169. It was not a success; the soldiers never got beyond an area around Dublin called "the Pale." Strongbow fell in love with an Irish girl, the daughter of one of the Irish kings, and married her.

Strongbow was not the last of his countrymen to fall in love with an Irishwoman. The stern Laws of Kilkenny passed in 1366 prohibited the English from marrying and having children with the Irish, and prohibited everyone from using any language except English and any but English names. They required "that every Englishman use the English custom, fashion, method of riding and clothes." The laws didn't work. The English and the Irish intermingled so completely that the English became "more Irish than the Irish."

During the Reformation much of Europe became Protestant, but Ireland, because of its isolation, remained Catholic. In an attempt to get control of the Irish, the English king, Henry VIII, proclaimed himself head of the Church of Ireland. But most of the Irish remained loyal to the Catholic Church and the Pope in Rome, so Henry, seeing the danger of an Irish revolt, ordered Parliament to declare him King of Ireland. In 1537 the English passed another law in an attempt to Anglicize the Irish, forbidding them to wear mustaches or shirts or caps dyed with an orange dye, insisting that they speak English, and finally making it law that they "shall keep their houses . . . as near as ever they can, according to the English order, condition, and manner."

When Henry's daughter Elizabeth became queen, she was as determined as her predecessors to get Ireland under control. She was prepared to be nasty about it: her deputy ordered that the heads of the rebels killed each day be cut off the bodies and laid next to the rebel's tent, as a terrifying lesson to the people who saw it. Apparently the tactic worked, for in 1602 the rebellious Irish were defeated at the Battle of Kinsale. The earls who had led the rebellion fled to Europe, in what was known as "The Flight of the Earls." Elizabeth was triumphant: the Irish rebels had been crushed at last.

The defeat marked the beginning of an important stage in the history of what would one day become Northern Ireland.

IV

COUNTY DOWN: CONQUERORS, COLONIZERS, AND ORDINARY PEOPLE

Queen Elizabeth I wanted to reward those English who had stood by her during her attempt to crush the rebellious Irish. She ordered Irish lands seized and given to loyal Englishmen, all members of the English aristocracy who also belonged to the Church of England. Known as the Ascendancy, these people were the landed gentry, the professionals, the privileged class. The new landlords had no intention of working the Irish farms themselves, so they imported farmworkers from Scotland or hired the displaced Irish to provide the labor. Some landlords got rid of their Scottish workers when they found the Irish would work for less money.

This was the beginning of the *plantation* of Ireland, a term used to describe the colonization process. King James I carried on what Elizabeth had begun, and in 1609 he began the full-scale plantation of Ulster, the northern province of Ireland. He brought in thousands of Scottish Lowlanders who swore an oath of loyalty to the English crown and received a grant of land in return. But from the beginning, the planters knew they were outnumbered by the native Catholic Irish, who were furious at having their land taken away.

In 1641, England was preoccupied with a civil war, and the Catholics of Ireland grabbed the chance to rebel. After the war ended in 1649, Oliver Cromwell was sent to Ireland to deal with the rebelling Catholics. He did it brutally, massacring the Irish without mercy and calling the large-scale killing "the righteous judgements and mighty works of God." Cromwell regarded the Irish as savages; his goal was to exterminate them.

Cromwell seized two and a half million acres of the best land not already in the hands of the English and Scots and used it to pay his soldiers. Many soldiers deserted and stayed in Ireland. Catholics who could prove they had not been involved in the rebellion were allowed to move to the western province of Connaught, the poorest farmland on the island.

By the middle of the seventeenth century the English Ascendancy was comfortably ensconced in Ireland, and Scottish and English Protestants had settled Ulster. Protestants built their homes on rolling farmlands with good soil and in coastal towns on broad plains with sandy beaches. Catholics, taking what was left, struggled to farm stony fields in rugged terrain. Their towns clung to wild coastlines with dangerous tides.

By this time the differences were clear between the lives of native and planter, Celt and Scot, Catholic and Protestant, and the foundation for the Troubles had been laid.

The Hamiltons' Farm

The Ards Peninsula fits the description of a Protestant landscape. The Ards is a narrow finger of land that crooks around Strangford Lough. A narrow road circles south along the seaside, passes through towns with names like Donaghadee, Ballywalter, and Portavogie, crosses the southern tip of the peninsula to Portaferry and then continues north along the lough to Greyabbey and Newtownards. It is part of County Down. Most of the Ards is farmland, rolling green fields with sturdy old stone houses. From most places you can see the sea to the east or the lough to the west.

Ruth Hamilton and her family live on a farm in the Ards midsection. She and her husband, Steven, both grew up within a mile or so of the old stone house in which they now live. The large house is thick-walled and square, set in the midst of lush lawns surrounded by neat hedges and flower gardens. There's a children's playhouse in a corner of the lawn, and a pair of white plaster lions crouch by the front door.

The setting is luxurious, but survival is a struggle for the Hamiltons. They own fifty acres on which a herd of dairy cattle grazes, but that's not a big enough farm to bring in a decent living. And so Ruth, like many of her neighbors, does "farmhouse accommodations," offering bed and breakfast to tourists. A faded signboard with the Tourist Board emblem hangs at the end of the long driveway. Ruth and Steven have moved into a smaller bedroom in the back of the house and fitted out the large front bedroom with a sink and an electric kettle for making tea. Breakfast comes with the price of the room.

Ruth invests time and energy taking her guests around to see the sights—when there are guests to take. Times are hard, a lot of farmers' wives have hung out signs, and competition is stiff. The Hamiltons' house has the disadvantage of being located on a side road that crosses the peninsula, and most tourists don't know it's there, so they stop instead at one of the guest houses in the village or along the sea road or the lough road.

There are other problems: Steven has a heart condition, and he may not be able to continue farming. The Hamiltons are thinking about leasing out the land to tenant farmers. In the meantime, Steven spends hours sprucing up the farm machinery to sell it.

The Hamiltons have two children. Janet, twelve, is deaf; Ruth had German measles when she was pregnant. Janet goes to a special school in Belfast where she has learned to read lips; she also carries a power pack strapped to her chest that greatly amplifies sound. The school, and the Hamiltons, are adamant that Janet not use sign language because that would take her out of the real world and limit her to the world of the deaf. They feel she must learn to communicate with people who are not deaf. But Ruth knows that Janet has picked up signing anyway; she's seen Janet use it with her friends at school.

Elaine, sixteen, short and overweight, was in the midst of her exams, but unlike most students I met who were tense and worried, Elaine seemed unconcerned. Her attitude disturbed her mother, who saw it not as confidence but as not caring. "Elaine has no drive, no direction," Ruth confided. "I don't know what's going to become of her."

Ruth cooked a large dinner, which was served in the dining room. Elaine had been appointed to set the table, using the good silver, but there were mistakes: she put the soup spoons where the dessert spoons belonged, or the other way around, and her mother sent her back to fix it. She protested a little, complained that it didn't matter, and finally did it right.

I assumed that the Hamiltons were Protestant. The names were the first indication, and the Ards Peninsula, with some of the best farmland in Ulster, is predominantly Protestant. It didn't take long to get into politics at the dinner table. Ruth said that the southern part of the peninsula is becoming increasingly Catholic.

"Why is that? Are the Protestants moving out?"

"No," she said, "it's the way they breed. The Catholics are outbreeding us, six or eight children in the family at least. Our families have only two or three."

I mentioned that I had been to hear Ian Paisley preach in Belfast. Steven, who told me that he's Presbyterian, has no time for Paisley. "He can call himself whatever he likes," Steven said flatly, "but he's not Presbyterian."

"But he's on our side, Daddy," Elaine argued.

"Doesn't matter," her father said.

I asked Steven if he were an Orangeman. "No, I'm not," he said. "I wouldn't say anything against the Orange Order, but I have no interest in it."

After dinner Elaine wanted to go to a meeting of the Young Farmers, possibly to avoid studying for exams. Ruth drove us to another farm and left us. It was a bad time for a meeting because so many students were involved in exams, but about fifteen Young Farmers gathered in the barnyard to learn the fine points of judging pigs. "Those two wee girls are Catholic," Elaine whispered, pointing to two girls perched on a fence rail.

Everybody was dressed in jeans and thick sweaters and high green boots called "wellies" (Wellingtons). They were carefully studying four sows with A, B, X, and Y marked on their broad backs. In a separate pen a single pig rooted in the straw. The young farmers all had score cards, and they were ranking the pigs according to a list of criteria: head and ears, spring of rib, topline and loin, hams. Next they were to appraise the single pig item by item, giving her points for things like the number and size of her teats, and then to present their opinion to the group.

I had a score card too, although my knowledge of pigs is limited to judging their appearance on a dinner plate. Despite my ignorance I joined in, finally selecting Pig X on the basis of her tail, which was much longer and curlier than the others. As it turned out, Pig X was indeed the best of the quartet, but her tail had nothing to do with it.

"Right pig, wrong reason," said a tall farmer with a distinctly Scottish accent, explaining that pigs raised indoors, as these were, are "docked," because they tend to chew each others' tails. The sow in the separate pen seemed to score high on the basis of grunts and squeals, but oinks were also not among the points listed for judging.

Before we left, the leader of the Young Farmers tried to enlist Elaine's help in a project for the group. She refused. "I'm not energetic," she explained, reinforcing her parents' frustrated view of her. That night, instead of "revising" for her exam the next day, she sat in her room and read, probably not a textbook, while her mother fretted in the kitchen about what would become of her lazy daughter.

Ruth and I made the rounds, stopping first at a community center to drop off huge pans of meat and vegetables that Ruth had cooked for the "pensioners' lunch." Several days a week elderly women in the area gather to visit, their knitting needles flying, and to enjoy a hot meal; Ruth is one of the volunteers who helps with the cooking. From there we called on her friend Mildred, a bubbly little woman who had prepared the rhubarb crumble for the lunch, trying to use up a bumper crop of rhubarb from her own garden. It is a lovely setting; the Irish Sea sparkled in the distance in a moment of sunshine. Mildred also operates a "farmhouse accommodation." Business is good, she said; too good. She'd like a break from it once in a while.

Next we visited a retired schoolteacher and a minister's widow. But this was Ruth's visit, not mine, and they spun a tangled web of conversation that did not include me. They talked rapidly in the local rising inflection, so that I didn't catch all that they were saying about people I didn't know, particularly a local boy who had just died, a schoolmate of Elaine's. Speculating on the cause of death—maybe asthma, maybe heart, maybe even drugs—they discussed his family and all his relations, near and distant.

It was very warm in that room, and I got drowsy from the heat and the endless rise and fall of their chatter that excluded me. A collection of fancy china plates hung on the wall above the sofa, and I counted twenty-nine of them, but thought that might be wrong and counted them again. Even after we were back in the car, Ruth continued the subject of family relationships, connecting everyone she knew with everyone else. I sensed that in spite of all this talk, Ruth is a lonely woman, troubled by worries about money, about Steven's health, about Janet's deafness, about Elaine's lackadaisical attitude.

Billy Burnside

Billy Burnside owns one of the best and most prosperous farms around. In the 1950s he and his wife, Evelyn, bought 112 unimproved acres, built a sturdy house on top of the hill with a sweeping view of Strangford Lough, put up the barns and outbuildings needed to raise sheep and beef cattle, and acquired another sixty acres. That's a big farm by Irish standards; most farms are even smaller than Steven Hamilton's marginal fifty acres. Ruth arranged for me to meet them. I was relieved when she said she had something else to do and would come for me later.

Silver cups and large trophies crowd a round table in the Burnsides' living room. Billy explained each of them, won by him and his two sons for excellence in various areas of farming. (His younger son, Wilson, was at the pig judging the day before.) The biggest trophies are "perpetual"—passed on each year—but since Billy has won them every year for the last six, they might as well be permanent.

Some of the awards belong to Billy's seventeen-year-old daughter Ann, now working in County Antrim. Evelyn brought out a piece of Ann's prize-winning stitchery work, an exquisitely smocked and embroidered dress that she worked on for two years. Her mother says she's also an excellent cook who hoped to use that skill professionally. Ann had done well in her exams when she was sixteen; her plan was to take the next level exams at eighteen, then go on to university to study home economics.

But Ann took a hard look at the future in a country where jobs are extremely scarce. A large company in County Antrim was looking for trainees, and even though Ann had no particular interest in the company or the kind of work being offered, she decided to go for an interview. She was one of twenty who were offered positions from among hundreds of applicants. And although she was barely seventeen she decided to take the job, rather than to continue her studies and face the prospect of not having *any* job available in another five years. Ann knew, too, that the possibility of getting a position she actually wanted was remote; better to take what was available now. It seems that the spectre of unemployment worries not only young people from working-class families, but from upper-middle-class families like the Burnsides as well.

"So now there you are," Billy said, and Evelyn offered tea. As usual it arrived with plates of cakes and cookies. Billy poured cream in his cup, settled back with his dogs at his feet, and said, "None of our problems is connected with religion. It has nothing to do with Protestants and Catholics."

I thought he meant—and was about to agree with him—that the conflict has little to do with what people actually believe about God or how they worship, that it has to do with the relationship between natives and colonizers, between the early Celts and the English and Scottish settlers who began to arrive in the seventeenth century. But that's not what Billy Burnside meant at all.

"It's *Communism*," he said. "It's a Communist plot, just like South Africa. The Pope wants a foothold here, in case the Commies take over Italy."

Since this was *not* what I thought, about either Northern Ireland or South Africa, I shut my mouth and smiled and accepted another piece of Evelyn's lemon cake. I was actually glad when Ruth Hamilton came to fetch me, and the women began talking and talking about people I didn't know.

V

COUNTY ANTRIM: QUIET TOWNS, PEACEFUL VILLAGES

Ballygilbert Grammar School

The place I have named Ballygilbert is a quiet country town a dozen or so miles north of Belfast; it feels like another world. The curbstones are painted red, white, and blue, and the pub by the bus stop is called The Red Hand, sure signs that I was in Protestant territory.

Mr. Magowan, the principal of the Ballygilbert Grammar School, tried to find a polite way to say that he didn't want the trouble of having a visitor, particularly an American writer, underfoot.

"It's unlikely that you'll find the children here much interested in the Troubles," he said, trying to head me off.

But in the end he agreed to let me come. The school was in the midst of a vast remodeling project, and it was difficult simply to get from one part of the building to another. I dodged a bucket outside the principal's door, which had a large sign with lights above it: ENTER—WAIT—ENGAGED. When I knocked, the WAIT light came on. Seconds later the light switched to ENTER. Magowan stood behind his desk, a tall man with a pencil-thin mustache, wearing a black academic robe. He passed me on to Miss Wilson, the career and guidance teacher.

She told me that Mr. Magowan had been brought to the school ten years ago when the place seemed to be falling apart. His job was to restore discipline. As part of that effort, students are required to dress in uniforms, and all teachers wear academic robes, except science teachers, who have white lab coats. Miss Wilson explained that the students I was about to meet were "first generation grammar school children" whose parents had attended high school or secondary school, not an elite grammar school like this one.

"Shall I stay with you then?" she asked. I was sure I'd get along just fine and said it might be better if I struggled alone to establish some kind of rapport. "But they like me," she protested. "They trust me. I'm sure my being there wouldn't make the slightest difference to them."

But I was sure that it would, and I tried politely to tell her that although it might not make any difference to the students, it did to me.

I was still in those first uncertain ten or fifteen minutes with three boys and four girls, still trying to find out who they were, how we could mesh, and what we were *really* going to talk about, when Miss Wilson appeared with a big smile and a tea tray. I had been asking some fairly innocuous questions, like what sort of town Ballygilbert was and why their families lived there (an indirect way of asking what kind of work their fathers did, which might have come across as a question about social status). Miss Wilson broke in, "Remember, you don't have to answer any questions unless you really want to." Of course then I felt like the Grand Inquisitor and was afraid to ask anything at all. Still, I managed to find out that two come from farming families, one father is a carpenter, another works for the weather station, a fifth father is retired from the Royal Air Force.

Miss Wilson had assured me that these students would claim to be completely unaffected by the Troubles, as she believed they really were. I didn't believe that *anybody* was "completely unaffected," even out here. Although Ballygilbert is only about twenty minutes by car from the city center, most of them rarely went into Belfast. An exception was Louise, whose mother was from the Shankill and still went to church there and was the leader of the Girls' Brigade. Louise was a junior leader and went along to help her mother —unless there had been some violence. Then they didn't want to endanger the GB's, and everyone stayed at home.

Michael, a square-jawed boy with short blond hair, claimed to be untouched by the Troubles, but he complained about security and the worthlessness of the handbag checks in some shops and public buildings. "Catholic women carry broken glass in their handbags, so security guards will cut their hands when they reach in," he said. "Now the guards wear gloves."

These students were in that comfortable breathing space between exams—the big ones would come next year. Most didn't know what they want to do after the exams, although a couple of the girls talked vaguely about art school. Only Michael seemed sure: he wants to go into the RAF, like his father, and he faces a stiff battery of tests for admission.

Miss Wilson did not leave after tea, and the conversation never really went anywhere. She gave me an "I-told-you-so" smile, put away the tea things, and offered me a lift back to Belfast.

Education in Northern Ireland operates on the English system. Children start school when they are five. Primary school pupils who have had their eleventh birthdays take a test called the "eleven-plus," an exam that may determine the course of their lives. The exam, given in the fall term, tests verbal reasoning and certain aspects of English and mathematics. Tests are geared so that about a quarter of the students will pass; those who pass go on to grammar schools, like Ballygilbert. Everyone else goes to high schools, sometimes called intermediate schools.

Grammar school is a seven-year course. At the end of the fifth year, when they're about sixteen, students take the "ordinary-level examinations," called "O-levels." Two years later they take the "advanced-level examinations" or "A-levels." A-levels are the equivalent of college entrance exams. Grammar school students who fail their O-levels usually find themselves in the much less prestigious intermediate school the following year. The exams themselves, given in May and June, are strenuous and stressful; students don't find out their grades—and the direction of their future—until mid-August.

Students I met in the midst of their O-levels were, with the exception of the directionless Elaine Hamilton in the Ards, nervous and tense. Teachers and parents didn't want me to take time away from the students' study schedule, and students themselves were conscious of the shortness of time and the pressure to do well. Each examination level is a kind of live-or-die situation that determines the course of your life: hit the top 25 percent in the eleven-plus and you're on track for a good education, straight through university—at government expense.

Grammar school gears its instruction toward the O- and A-levels. Do well on those two, and you can pick your university in Northern Ireland or elsewhere in the United Kingdom. But children who aren't good at taking tests, or who may not have hit their stride academically by the age of eleven, will find themselves on a totally different track, labeled "less able." Although late-bloomers can make a comeback and survive and thrive in a less academically oriented school—and many do—it's not easy. Intermediate school pupils take exams and are granted general certificates. And many leave school at sixteen without passing any exams or earning any certificates, some to go to work but many more to go on the Bru.

Practically all Protestants attend "state schools," supported entirely by the government. Practically all Catholics attend church schools that get most, but not all, of their support from government funds. This is one of the important ways in which children are kept apart and taught separateness. It is not simply in the matter of religious education that they are different; Catholics and Protestants learn different versions of the history of their country: the Catholics from the perspective of the native and the Protestants from that of the colonizer.

When segregation in U. S. schools was finally brought to an end, some Americans began to say that it wasn't enough simply to end segregation—it was necessary to push for integration in order to expose young people to each other, to let them get to know each other as human beings.

But that's not the way it is in Northern Ireland. Not only do most people live in segregated areas that keep Catholics and Protestants apart, but they send their children to separate schools. Occasionally, some parents decide that their children ought to attend one of the few integrated schools in Northern Ireland, believing that people truly committed to peace and reconciliation can begin by educating their children in the same schools. But such schools, and such parents, are rare, and the cost in human terms is stiff: priests have been known to refuse communion to parents whose children attend integrated schools, and bishops have refused to confirm the children.

Catholics and Protestants go to different schools, play different sports, learn different games, and sing different songs. Their exams—eleven-plus, O-level, A-level—are one thing all students share.

School for Farmers

Northern Ireland has two universities—Queen's University in Belfast and the University of Ulster—and twenty-six "Institutions of Further Education" that include teachers' colleges and technical schools. One day I drove out to one of these technical schools, an agricultural college in a rich farming area. The man who suggested I go there, and who made the first contact for me, was Ernie Phillips, the farmer from County Down who had also warned me that I might run into suspicion, or at least some wariness.

I found neither. People were cordial. During lunch in the cafeteria, a teacher named Bruce quietly rounded up some students he thought I'd like to meet and found us an empty room. The students seemed pleased to talk about their families, their farms, their plans. Laura, who wore a sweater from her boyfriend's school, does not aspire to run the family farm. "I have an older sister and two brothers ahead of me," she said, "but I like working with animals."

"Who gets the farm?" is always the big question. At lunch Bruce had told me that few farmers make wills or hand over their farms to the next generation, because that would be accepting their own mortality, facing the fact that they will one day die.

"The boy who really wants the farm tends to do poorly in school," Bruce said. "That shows clearly that he is sincere; he *really* wants it. Boys who are good students might change their minds and go off and do something else." That kind of attitude gives schools like this one a tough challenge: teaching them what they need to know in order to be good farmers, but understanding that they resist working for good grades because that might send the wrong message to their fathers.

The students complained to me that school is too theoretical—but they admitted they are learning good practical techniques.

"Like what?" I asked.

"Well, that dehorning is better done at two months than at four," red-haired Colin said, "and that there are ways to castrate cattle more humanely."

"Then the problem," said Laura, "is to convince your father that you've learned a better way."

"They don't want to hear about new techniques," Bob complained. "They'll tell you they've done it this way all their lives, and if it's worked out all along there's no need to change now. They're stiff-necked. Really stubborn."

"What we need," Laura said, "is a course in psychology, to teach us how to teach our fathers to accept what we've learned."

They complained, too, about the high cost of farmland, now the equivalent of $2200 to $4500 an acre, an investment that makes it almost impossible for them *ever* to buy their own farms. (They measure the size of their parents' farms in terms of head of cattle—usually 100 or more—rather than by acreage, which may include rented land.) Add to that the problem of keeping up with the neighbors: they told stories of farmers who have gone hopelessly into debt buying expensive equipment and putting up costly buildings. They joked about the five-year plans they're required to draw up as a class project, plans that would bankrupt any farmer who tried to follow them, partly because of high interest rates on borrowed money.

After a while the conversation drifted from farming to other subjects—drugs, for example, primarily cannabis, as they call marijuana, because they're totally unfamiliar with anything else. Laura, for instance, who went to Ballygilbert Grammar School, said she has been offered cannabis at parties in Belfast, but that's relatively uncommon. On the other hand, they told me, *everybody* drinks and *everybody* smokes cigarettes.

In another jog in the conversation, a student named Jimmy offered his family as living proof that the Bru can provide a satisfactory standard of living: he is the middle child of *seventeen* children; his father decided at the age of fifty-five to retire and pass his job on to his oldest son. With all those dependents, the weekly payments from the Bru are high, and the family lives well.

I knew that this was a mixed group—the names, the schools, the size of the families showed it. Bruce had said that at this level students get along well. "They discuss politics," he said, "and sometimes it gets hot. But never violent. The violent ones are weeded out early on."

We didn't get into politics, but I did ask what would happen if they brought home boyfriends or girlfriends of the "other" religion. They all hooted. There would be hell to pay, they said.

"It's not so much that our parents themselves would disapprove," Laura explained. "But our parents are all afraid of what their friends would say."

The Antrim Coast

Tourists flock to the Antrim Coast, escaping depressing, industrial Belfast and heading north along the narrow road that winds along the sea. It is a rugged and beautiful area, and one Sunday—it was my birthday and I had given myself a day off—I drove slowly along the coast. I stopped when I felt like it to gaze out across the water, trying for a glimpse of Scotland, at one point only twelve miles across the misty North Channel. It was windy and cool but not raining, a "nice day" in Irish terms. Listen to the names of the towns I drove through: Portrush, Bushmills, Ballyclare, Cushendun, Cushendall, Carnlough, Glenarm, Ballygally. "Bally" means "town land" and is a common place name; other place names begin with "castle" or with "dun" or "down," which means there had been a fort there.

I had spent the night before in a hotel by the sea, indulging myself in a room with its own bathroom ("After all it's my birthday, and here I am a million miles from home") and a good dinner. I ordered local prawns and a thick steak and watched the sun descend behind the headlands of distant Donegal. The trouble was I had to watch the sunset alone, and I was suddenly very lonely.

But the people at the next table were cordial, and before the prawn cocktail was gone we were engaged in a lively conversation. When the steak arrived I noticed that the waitress had a rather large tattoo on her forearm, and I remembered the boy in Seamus's class talking about the "millies" with their rough, hard ways. I mentioned the tattoo to the couple at the next table. The woman stared at me. "Are you a writer?" she asked.

I wondered if I should apologize for it. "How did you know?"

"You're eccentric," she said. "You travel on your own, you notice everything, and you ask a lot of questions."

We talked a little more, about books and writing but not about tattooed waitresses, and the couple left. I settled down grumpily to face the evening alone.

The lounge was crowded with people who had come to listen to a local folksinger. All the tables were full, but a woman invited me to join her and her husband. Helen was a tall, elegant woman in a smart orange suit; Roland was handsome and graying at the temples. I promised myself I would not mention tattoos or ask a lot of questions or let on that I am a writer.

I talked about my life in Albuquerque, and they talked about their town. "It's peaceful here. Everyone gets along. The Troubles don't affect us," Roland said.

"We have a wee girl of eight, Louise, and she's never even *heard* of terrorists," Helen said. "She reads fairy tales about knights and kings and castles, not about people throwing stones and petrol bombs."

It came as a relief that life is peaceful here. In this place the winter winds are so fierce that Roland seals the front door shut in the fall and doesn't open it again until spring. I had followed the "Nun's Walk" along the beach to the Promenade where tourist coaches were parked, and shops and restaurants were humming with elderly people on holiday. Helen and Roland once owned a restaurant here; they sold it, took a year off, and opened a shop. They seemed content.

The folksinger took a break and came over to say hello. His name was John McNally, and he was their next-door neighbor. Naturally I picked up on the names—Helen and Roland would be Protestant, and McNally was surely a Catholic. But neighbors and friends! I felt hopeful. John finished his pint of ale and began strumming his guitar again under a spotlight. He sang a series of cowboy and country songs for the tourist from New Mexico, including "Waltz Across Texas," one state away, but close enough for someone feeling slightly homesick. Then he got everyone—the whole roomful—to sing "Happy Birthday." (I *had* mentioned that.)

The next morning I started my slow drive back to Belfast along the Antrim Coast, stopping first at the Giant's Causeway, a geological phenomenon created by the cooling of a lava formation into some 38,000 separate rock pipes. It's a place where myths flourish. For instance, there's the story of the first legendary O'Neill who sailed toward Ulster from Scotland out of the murky mists of ancient history. He was one of several contenders for the island; the first one to get there could claim it. According to writer Leon Uris, when O'Neill came within sight of land, he cut off his hand and hurled it onto the shore, thus staking his claim. That, says Uris, is the source of the Red Hand of Ulster, one of the strongest Unionist symbols. No one I talked to in Northern Ireland knew that story, but they all liked the goriness of it.

A harsh wind blasted the Giant's Causeway. It was on my climb back up to the cliff that I met the traveler with the Canadian red maple leaf on his backpack. He was on his way to Ballygally and he needed a lift. I offered to take him along provided he was in no hurry and would put up with my preference for back roads and my frequent stops. He agreed.

He was from Edmonton, Alberta, and had been traveling for about five weeks, the start of a "megatour" to last at least a year, or as long as money and stamina held out. We took a walk back through one of the spectacular Antrim glens with plunging waterfalls and stopped in a pretty seaside village where the whole town seemed to be out strolling, heading for a sweet shop for "sliders"—ice cream sandwiches.

I never asked him his name, and he didn't ask me mine. It turned out that he knew something about me, though; he had stayed in a B&B run by the wife of a teacher at a school I had visited, and the teacher had mentioned the American writer. If not a small world, then certainly a small country. He talked about his experiences and impressions so far, and I talked about mine. We were the outsiders.

"They say they're unaffected by the Troubles here."

"Do you believe it?"

"No. Do you?"

"No. The Troubles are everywhere in Northern Ireland. But some places do have less violence."

N
Portstewart
Coleraine
Lough Foyle
Letterkenny
DONEGAL
Londonderry
LONDONDERRY
River Foyle
SPERRIN MOUNTAINS
Strabane
Maghera
Donegal
Cookstown
Omagh
Lower Lough Erne
TYRONE
Lough Neagh
Dungannon
FERMANAGH
Enniskillen
Portadown
Upper Lough Erne
Armagh
ARMAGH
LEITRIM
WESTERN NORTHERN IRELAND
Miles
0
20
0
20
Kms.
©1987 A.Karl/J.Kemp

VI

COUNTY TYRONE: NON-CATHOLICS AND NON-PROTESTANTS

More than sixteen million Americans are of Irish descent. I am not one of them. As far as I know, none of my ancestors came from Ireland. Most people I met casually in Northern Ireland assumed I was there either to visit "relations" or to trace my ancestry, a favorite activity of American tourists.

The people of Northern Ireland on both sides of the sectarian fence could not figure out what a person named "Meyer" was. I explained that my ancestors were German. Had I been to that German village, then, to seek my roots? They found it hard to believe that my curiosity about my family extends back only to my grandparents and a few old photographs of *their* parents.

I was born in central Pennsylvania, an area with a large number of people of German descent. That wasn't something you bragged about when I was growing up in the 1940s and America was at war with Germany. What I never noticed until I began reading about Northern Ireland were the place names: my childhood home was in Derry Township; the township next to ours was Armagh, about an hour's drive from Tyrone—Ulster names.

Those names were brought to Pennsylvania by a migration in the eighteenth century of some quarter million Ulstermen whose ancestors had moved from Scotland to the northern part of Ireland in the seventeenth century at the invitation of King James I. But when Ulster was dominated by the English Ascendancy, wealthy Church of Ireland people, the Presbyterian farmers who had been "planted" there found themselves almost as badly off as the Irish Catholics. Protestants—that is, the English Ascendancy—ruled firmly from Dublin, where the Irish Parliament was under the tight control of the English King. Irish-Protestant businessmen were not allowed to trade freely, since laws protected English businessmen from Irish competition. Other laws made life as miserable for Presbyterians as it did for Catholics, who were forbidden to own land, hold office, or worship freely.

Beginning around 1700 and over the next century, the Ulster Scots left Ireland for America, where they were called the "Scotch-Irish." A stern, hard-working group, the new arrivals immediately went to work in their adopted country and quickly made their mark on it. By 1776 there were 123 Ulster settlements in America. One of these Ulster emigrants was Thomas Mellon, born in County Tyrone in 1813 in a thatched cottage built by his father. When Thomas was five years old the Mellon family left for America; he worked his way to success as a banker and judge in Pittsburgh, Pennsylvania. His son Andrew was one of the wealthiest men in America. The little whitewashed cottage in County Tyrone became the focal point of the Ulster-American Folk Park, a celebration of the "American connection," Ulster's particular ties with the young United States.

The Northern Ireland Tourist Board has a poster map that shows every American connection they could find. Frontiersmen like Davy Crockett and Sam Houston, writers like F. Scott Fitzgerald and Edgar Allan Poe, songwriter Stephen Foster, soldiers like Stonewall Jackson were all of Ulster ancestry. Five Ulstermen signed the Declaration of Independence, the poster advises, and a man from Strabane, County Tyrone, printed it and went on to establish the first daily newspaper in America. Two of our early men in space, John Glenn and Neil Armstrong, trace their roots to Ulster.

But the most boasted-about of the Ulster-American Who's Who is the list of presidents, described in a glossy publication titled "From Here to the White House." Never mind John Fitzgerald Kennedy and Ronald Reagan—their ancestors came from the South and emigrated at a later time. We're noting here only the men of Ulster: Andrew Jackson, James Buchanan, and Chester Alan Arthur were all first-generation Americans, the sons of Ulstermen. The ancestral home of Ulysses S. Grant in County Tyrone bears a plaque. In that same county is yet another thatched cottage that claims to have been the birthplace of a president's grandfather; the grandson was Woodrow Wilson. The farm is still owned and being worked by Wilson "relations." So far eleven of our presidents have been proved to have Ulster roots, and genealogists are still working on Monroe, Truman, and Eisenhower.

But there is another Ulster-American connection that interested me more than the ancestry of great Americans. That was the group of teenagers in County Tyrone who were preparing to spend a month in the United States as part of Channels of Peace. Every summer hundreds—some say thousands—of young people, from children through young adults, leave Northern Ireland for other countries, some strictly for the holiday but many as part of various peace and reconciliation schemes. An equal number of Catholics and Protestants, boys and girls, are brought together in a group aimed at some kind of mutual understanding. Out of Northern Ireland in a different environment, many of these young people for the first time in their lives have the freedom to make friends with other young people across sectarian lines without fear of reprisal—no one will beat them up or badmouth them. The idea, then, is that they'll learn from experience that the "others" are real people, perhaps more like them than different. By staying with host families in the United States (some groups go to Norway, Germany, and other European countries), they can see how people in other countries live peacefully despite religious differences.

I went to meet Channels of Peace people in County Tyrone a month before their departure, while they were still getting themselves organized. I wanted to learn something about their community, their schools, churches, youth organizations, and their families.

I knew nothing about Lewistown—my name for the place—but I had picked from a guidebook a small hotel on the main street as my headquarters for a few days. I was ready for a change from B&Bs with the owner knowing exactly what I was doing at every moment, and monitoring all my phone calls and visitors.

The problem was, I couldn't seem to find the main street. No wonder. It is a tightly controlled security area, sealed off to vehicles except through one checkpoint where ruddy-cheeked young soldiers search your car if they think you look like a security risk. Apparently my American accent or my American face got me through without a search. I parked the car long enough to check into the hotel, and an employee came to guide me out of the security zone, through a maze of streets, and finally to the protected car park behind the hotel.

I was given a room on the third floor facing the main street, which was three blocks long and going nowhere, with the town hall at one end obscured by a high security fence. I liked the chance to observe street life from my window until someone reminded me it was safer to be in the back of the hotel. When bombs go off—as they had at this hotel, three or four times—you really don't want to be near a front window.

Father Paul

"You are very welcome," said the chubby man with blond Shirley Temple ringlets. Father Paul was one of several priests on the staff at St. Mary's Roman Catholic Church, and organizing the Lewistown branch of Channels of Peace was one of the many responsibilities he juggled. But Father Paul is a born juggler. I had no sooner settled in my hotel room than he rang up to say that he had rounded up some teenagers, and they were all waiting for me in the hotel conference room.

He wanted me to tell the peace-project people who I was, what I was doing there, and how I planned to do it. We moved the chairs out of formal rows and into a haphazard circle, and there I was again, facing a room full of faces, some bored, some curious, trying to find a way to open up a line of communication between us. Father Paul asked me what it's like to be a writer. One of the parents in the room asked why I was writing the book. I tried to explain. More questions, more explanations.

Not everybody in the room was headed for the same place in the U.S.; they would scatter to several cities. All were fifteen, all at the end of their fifth year in the seven-year grammar school course, and all consumed that week by the dread O-level exams. It would be hard to pry them loose from their studying to do much talking. Father Paul asked me after the meeting what I was interested in.

"People," I said.

"That makes it easier," he said. "There isn't much to do here. I assume you've already seen *Out of Africa*. I'll see what I can arrange for you."

For the next several days I struggled to keep up with him and all the things he thought I should do, the places I should go, the people I should meet.

Rob Ross

"I failed me driving test," Rob said sadly. "First the examiner didn't like the way I handled the gears, and then I was going down the hill there from the church, and this little old lady comes out from between some cars and steps right in front of me! I nearly hit her, I did. The examiner said I didn't brake fast enough, so he failed me. And it was really her fault."

It was a disappointing day in Rob's life, but in the next few days we spent so much time together that I finally got him to joke about it. "It was probably a policeman dressed up like an old lady," I told him. "They just didn't want you out on the road."

Rob, barely nineteen, was facing heavy responsibility as the youth leader for one of the Channels of Peace groups. Most of the other leaders, although a few years older, were also uneasy about the prospect of watching over a group of sixteen teenagers: eight boys and eight girls, eight of them Protestant, eight Catholic. Some would be away from home for the first time—it was Rob's first time, too—and in a foreign country. I didn't blame Rob for being nervous.

He's a tall, gangly young man with sharp features, pale blue eyes, and a reticent smile. Bit by bit I learned things about him: that he worked in a grocery store, having recently dropped out of a technical course he thought was too theoretical and bookish; that he has two younger sisters at home and his mum does some part-time child care; that he is Protestant. Lewistown has a population of some 22,000, about 60 percent Catholic, but Rob has not known many Catholics; all this interaction with Catholics was a totally new experience for him. Riding in a car with a priest was a first; so was visiting the parochial house where Father Paul and the priests of St. Mary's live. (Straitlaced Rob was agape at Paul's collection of good French wines; he insisted that CofI ministers never touch alcohol, although I knew differently.)

But the most important thing I learned about him was that in 1979, when Rob was twelve, his father was standing at the end of a country lane waiting for a ride to work and was shot to death by members of the IRA.

"I remember when they came and told me Davy Ross had been killed," Father Paul said. "I had just finished saying mass. I remember the gospel I read that morning. It was a terrible thing. Davy Ross was well-liked in this town. He had a garage and fixed cars. Everyone knew him."

"Why did they kill him?"

"A lot of people ask that question. I think Rob asks that question every day. Davy had friends on both sides. He wasn't political, but he did work for the Ulster Defence Regiment. He wasn't even a member of the UDR; he just did some part-time maintenance work on their vehicles. But somebody hated him for that."

The UDR—Ulster Defence Regiment—is the local army, made up of recruits from Northern Ireland, almost all Protestant. There is a UDR garrison not far from Lewistown; the garrison of the British army is also in the area. Both military groups are hated by the IRA. (The UDR is not to be confused with the UDA, an illegal paramilitary group.)

"You never think it can happen to you," Rob said, "and then it does. The bitterness doesn't go away. It's still there."

Dances and Wakes

On my first night in Lewistown Father Paul announced that he would pick me up about 9:30; there were places he wanted to take Rob and me. That seemed a little late to be starting out, but life in Northern Ireland beats at a different tempo. At this latitude it doesn't get dark until very late in the summer, and so it was still broad daylight when we left.

Father Paul's life is a round of ceremonial appearances as parish priest, and he was taking us to a tiny community some ten miles from Lewistown where he had to present awards and trophies to bowls teams at the annual dance. (Bowls is a game similar to bowling, played on a lawn.) Music was being provided by a County Tyrone group called Paddy and the Chandeliers. ("They hang together," Father Paul said.) The dance was to begin at nine, but when we drove by around ten o'clock, the band had not yet arrived.

To pass the time, Father Paul took us on a tour, down humpbacked lanes walled in with tall, dense hedges clipped as smooth as flat-top haircuts. They formed a tunnel so narrow two cars could not pass.

"They're Protestant hedges," he said. "You can always tell." He turned down a road where unclipped hedges sprawled in a tangle. "Now we're in Catholic territory. As you can see." We passed a farmhouse surrounded by pristine lawns. "A Jewish family from America," he explained. "Why in God's name would a Jew want to live in this crazy country?"

We climbed a hill, leaving the farms below; the land up here was all bog, a source of peat that is widely used for fuel.

Ten percent of Ireland is covered with a thick layer of partially decomposed plant life; with enough time and pressure the peat, also called turf, would become coal. Here in the country people dig the blocks of peat and stack them on racks to dry before they are burned. In some places peat is harvested mechanically and compressed into briquets. Although peat produces only half as much heat as coal when it burns, it is used to generate electricity and is what most people use to heat their homes in a country lacking both wood and coal.

Darkness had finally settled over the countryside by the time we got back to the parish hall and found a place to leave the car. Cars were parked every which way; drivers in Northern Ireland do not park cars so much as *abandon* them. Inside the hall Paddy and the Chandeliers, decked out in vests and string ties, were cranking out a kind of Irish oom-pah. The dance floor was jammed with middle-aged people in their best clothes—men in jackets and neckties, women in summery dresses—gracefully executing the turns of a fast waltz. Our arrival attracted attention: Father Paul, the popular priest, in clerical garb; Rob by far the youngest person present and recognized by many as a Prod and Davy Ross's son; and a woman with an American face dressed inappropriately in jeans (I was thinking of country and western dances at home when I put them on, and I was dead wrong).

It was now 11:30 on a weeknight, and the evening was just getting underway. They were not ready yet for Father Paul to award the prizes stacked on the stage next to Paddy's amps. He would have time to make another call with us: Mr. Flannery's wake.

"Not me favorite kind of music," Rob said as we drove off.

Dressed in a dark suit and white shirt, Niall Flannery was laid out in his wooden hex-shaped coffin on the bed he had slept on all of his married life, a rosary twined among his waxy fingers. His coffin was strewn with sympathy cards and surrounded by sweet-smelling flowers, and the coffin lid with a crucifix in the center leaned against the wall of the bedroom. His puffy-eyed widow in black sat at the foot of the bed. She had been there without sleep for more than a day and intended to remain at her place all through the night. The funeral would be at St. Mary's in the morning.

Rob and I trailed after Father Paul, who exchanged greetings with dozens of Mr. Flannery's friends, relatives, and neighbors milling about downstairs, the women fussing over platters of food, the men smoking outside. Mourners took turns in the straight chairs lined up around the walls of the bedroom. Father Paul spoke sympathetically with the new widow about the unexpectedness of the death—there had been no sign of heart trouble, had there?—and introduced Rob and me.

I could sense Rob's discomfort. This was a Catholic housing estate that Rob Ross had never entered before and where, without Father Paul's protection, he would not be safe. His presence did not go unnoticed. "I overheard people whispering, 'Isn't that Davy Ross's boy?' Rob probably wondered if one of the men in that roomful of people was the one who killed his father," Father Paul said to me later. "He's decided to go to mass with me tomorrow. He'll be required to go as part of Channels of Peace when he's in America, and he wants to start practicing now."

Sometime after 1:00 A.M. Father Paul dropped me off at my hotel. His night was only beginning. From there he went back to the bowls party and had just managed to give away all the prizes by 2:00 A.M. when the electricity failed and the lights went out. Candles were rustled up for the last number, which Paddy and the Chandeliers performed without amps. Everyone else went home "early," but Father Paul returned to the wake, where the serious drinking had begun. He stayed until 5:00 P.M., got a couple of hours of sleep, and began his day by laying to rest the soul of Niall Flannery.

* * *

"I must be completely daft to be doing this," Rob muttered from the backseat of Father Paul's car. Paul was taking us for a drive through the countryside to a village that is almost completely Catholic. Here the curbs were painted green, white, and orange, the colors of the Republic, and the Irish tri-color fluttered from the tops of several flagpoles. (It is all right to fly the tri-color unless someone complains that it is an "act of provocation," which someone almost always does, except in this town.) "Up the IRA" graffiti appeared on several walls, this time without the usual Prod response, "Fuck the Pope."

Only one Union Jack was in evidence, barely visible above a police barracks built like a fortress with some eighty RUC men virtually sealed behind its thick concrete walls and miles of barbed wire. Helicopters whirred in and out. The helicopters, which belong to the army, are the only means left for patrolling the area. Even in an armored patrol car an RUC man runs a real risk of being dead before he reaches the end of the street. The police force as a community service, responding to calls for burglaries or traffic accidents, no longer exists in places like this. Father Paul had some strong feelings about it.

"There's always confusion when police take on military authority, as they have here," he said. "They ought to acknowledge that they're paramilitary and not a community service. We've driven past the barracks twice now. They probably have a helicopter tracking us."

"Daft," Rob groaned.

Lewistown Schools

"Schools," Father Paul announced on the telephone. I had completely turned my time over to him. He seemed to know everybody in the community, and it was a relief not to have to figure out everything myself. "I got you into as many as I could, which is two. Catholic grammar school in the morning, state intermediate school in the afternoon." He gave me directions, names, times. "Look after yourself," he said, the equivalent of "take care," and hung up.

Sister Brigid at St. Mary's Grammar School was in charge. She had decided to make maximum use of my presence and arranged for me to meet four of her classes during the morning. I had become a sort of visiting lecturer, valued for bringing in an outside view, trusted to be noncontroversial, but standing in front of a class was not useful to *me*.

This was a grammar school, the intellectual elite, all girls. The older girls were serious, pondering each subject we discussed, but the younger ones were exuberant, interrupting each other to tell me about the play they wrote and performed, to ask if I would send them a copy of the book, to request my autograph. They were full of questions.

"Are you looking for terrorists?" they asked. I said if I saw one I'd probably run the other way.

"Were you expecting to see fighting on every street corner?" They see their town as peaceful, and for this violent country, it *was* peaceful—or it was then. There had been plenty of violence in the past. But they don't even notice the signs of violence they've grown up with: the barricaded roads, the security checks, the fortresslike police station.

I told them about the near-error Father Paul made when he delivered me to my hotel the previous night; he had inadvertently left on his headlights while he escorted me from the car park in the rear to the front door, and we had been pursued by a shouting security guard. Father Paul skipped back to kill the lights, explaining that a car left with its lights on was a signal that it was rigged with a bomb. If the guard had not happened to notice Father Paul, the army bomb squad would have been called and the entire neighborhood—including the hotel—evacuated. That may not be the same as "fighting on every street corner," but in my view it qualified as a sign of the kind of tension that accompanies violence waiting to happen.

"What do you think of Northern Ireland so far?" the students asked. I evaded the question with jokes about the weather, a safer topic. I couldn't tell them that I thought their country was sad and depressing.

Father Paul wanted me to have the "Complete Lewistown Experience," which meant eating lunch in the cafeteria at St. Mary's. After the girls murmured grace, the head girl at each table brought out a tray loaded with serving dishes containing the usual colorless, tasteless meal: peas and carrots cooked to mush, piles and piles of mashed potatoes, an unidentifiable substance with a white sauce to pour over it. My guess was some sort of fish loaf, but I couldn't prove it, and neither could Sister Brigid.

What can I say about Lewistown's secondary school? Rob was a graduate, and he went with me. We followed a teacher named Miss Haddon from building to building, ducking in and out of a downpour. "Don't expect much," she said over her shoulder. "These children are quiet and reserved. They won't talk to you."

"Don't worry," I said confidently. "I always manage to get them to talk to me about *something*."

Wrong.

Thirty young teenagers sat poker-faced behind their desks and stared me down. The girls wore their hair cut very short, and all the students dressed in school uniforms, white shirts with neckties, so that I couldn't tell girls from boys unless I peered under the desk to see if they were wearing skirts or pants. Nothing worked. I used my usual ice-breaker, describing experiences I'd had writing other books like the one about Eskimos and their strange food. When I tried to make eye contact, they looked away, afraid I'd ask them something. I could not coax a single response out of them. Miss Haddon sat in the back, under orders from the principal not to leave the room. I understood his policy, but I was sure I'd fare better without her. What made it even worse was Rob back there watching me expectantly, waiting for me to charm the class.

At last there came a lone, tentative question: "Do you know any cowboys?"

Father Paul met us as we stepped dejectedly out of the school building into the pouring rain. "There's one more experience you must not miss," he said. "Riding a school bus."

He had arranged for me to go home with one of the girls from St. Mary's, and he dropped me off at the bus station to meet Clare O'Connor. "Part of the experience," he said cheerily, "is waiting in the rain."

Clare O'Connor

Every day hundreds of school children gather at the bus station, sorting themselves out by tribe, Protestants at one end, Catholics at the other. Buses generally transport one or the other, but a few of them are integrated. In Lewistown "integrated" means that, on the double-decker buses, Catholics are on the top deck and Protestants on the bottom on the way to school in the morning and then reversed for the trip home. Or, for the smaller bus that Clare and I took, RCs sit in front and Prods in the back.

When the bus pulled into the station we jumped on and

scrambled for seats. It was not a long trip, thank goodness, not more than fifteen minutes or so. There was no conversation between the two groups. The Catholics were loud and rowdy, and the Protestants in the back maintained a stony silence. "Is it always like this?" I whispered to Clare.

"We outnumber them," she said. "Then they're quiet as mice. But when there are more of them, *they* are the ones to carry on."

Clare's father, Conor O'Connor, had come home early from work. He and his youngest son, Ciaran, were assembling a plastic model at the kitchen table. The other children, Roisin (ro-SHEEN) and Kevin, hung around watching and waiting for their after-school snack. Their older brother, Patrick, was away in England, studying at Oxford. Their mother had put on the kettle for tea, but "tea" that day turned out to include cold chicken, ham, cheeses, bread, and eggs, and ended with a wonderful concoction called "Pavlova," a meringue shell filled with fruit and whipped cream.

The thing uppermost on Conor O'Connor's mind that day was Irish boxer Barry McGuigan who had a bout coming up in Las Vegas, Nevada, the following month. Conor had traveled to all the champ's fights around the British Isles, and he was planning to go to the States for this one, too. McGuigan, Conor said, is a Catholic from the South who married a Protestant girl and moved to Northern Ireland so that he could have British citizenship and a British passport, feeling it would help him in his career. (It didn't help his match, though; McGuigan was soundly beaten by a boxer from Texas.)

A few years ago Conor and his wife, Ethna, went to Florida on a holiday; they enjoyed it so much that they came home and told the children that if everyone saved carefully for two years, they'd go back and take the whole family. Last summer all seven O'Connors descended on Disneyworld, Epcot Center, Sea World, the works. "We've seen the best part of America now," Clare said. "Everything else would probably be a letdown after Florida." I said I thought there were other parts they might enjoy, too.

After Conor has come back from Las Vegas, the family plans to leave for a summer holiday at their cottage on a tiny island off the coast of Donegal, to the northwest. It's the only house on the island, a simple place without electricity. They take all their food and supplies with them from home, except bread and milk; food and almost everything else is much cheaper in Northern Ireland than it is in the Republic.

My feet were wet, as usual, and Clare put my shoes on a radiator to dry. She was still in her school uniform from St. Mary's, a dull-brown V-neck sweater over a white shirt and a short straight skirt. She made another pot of tea, ignoring her father's teasing about not knowing how to do it properly. We talked about the weather, of course, because that was always the safest subject to begin with.

This led to farming matters. County Tyrone is a major area for growing grass to feed cattle that are exported all over the world. Animals were already starving, Conor said. Cows had to be kept in barns so they wouldn't sink in the muddy fields, which were too soft to support them. It was impossible to harvest the grass for silage. The grass hadn't grown well because there was so little sunshine, and now it was too wet to cut. This was the second summer of nonstop rain in Ulster; the year before was also a disaster. People talked about another famine. "If it keeps up, we'll be asking the Ethiopians for money," Conor said darkly. His children were properly shocked.

"We judge the weather by the number of gigantic jigsaw puzzles we put together while we're on holiday," Ethna said. "Usually we don't finish even one. Last year we finished two and could have done another one."

The O'Connors obviously live well, and money tends to isolate people from the Troubles. But not entirely. Ethna remembers hearing the shots on the day Davy Ross was killed. She likes young Rob, although she doesn't know him well. "He could have gone either way," she said. "He could have become a violent, antisocial Catholic-hater. But instead he's turning out to be a remarkable young man."

Money doesn't isolate people from prejudice and bigotry. Conor O'Connor is a prosperous businessman who owns a large, well-kept country property. "This is one of the last Catholic farms on the road out of town," he said. "From here on they're all Protestant. I tried to buy one of those Protestant farms, and I actually bid £2,000 more than the man who got it. But the night before the sale the auctioneer came to me and told me he had been instructed not to sell it to me, no matter how much I bid."

Conor told the story of the wealthy Catholic solicitor (as lawyers are called), who was determined to buy eighty acres of prime farmland owned by a Protestant. He had a solicitor in England make the purchase and then turn it over to him. "That's the kind of thing that causes a lot of bad feeling around here. Of course it goes the other way as well—Catholics won't sell to Prods."

I asked how Clare got involved in Channels of Peace and how she was chosen to go. Deirdre O'Mally had told me in Belfast that teenagers with leadership ability were hand-picked so that they would influence their own groups when they came home again. But that wasn't how it worked for Clare.

"Father Donovan over at St. Mary's had all of us who were interested put our names in a bowl, one for the boys and one for the girls, and then he drew out four names from each one. I never thought I'd get to go, but I made a novena to St. Jude, the patron saint of hopeless causes, and two weeks later the names were drawn and mine was one of them. I was so excited! But then I found out they had made a mistake of some kind, and they had to do the drawing all over again. There was no time for a special novena—that takes nine days—but I just prayed and prayed to St. Jude, and my name was drawn the second time, too. It was just like a miracle!"

The conversation was beginning to try the patience of little Roisin, in thick glasses, the spoiled baby of the family. She had been trying to break in, with no luck. Clare kept shushing her. Roisin made one more try: "What's black and white and bounces?" she demanded.

Nobody knew.

"A rubber nun," she said.

Colm Gillespie and the Protestants

Two Protestant families had invited me to call, one for morning tea and one for lunch, the families of girls who were going to America. It was Father Paul's idea to send Colm Gillespie along as chauffeur. Colm is a schoolteacher and Catholic youth leader with the project, and the two girls, Susan Montgomery and Jane Hunter, were in his group bound for Blue River. It would be a good chance for me to get acquainted with Colm, Father Paul said, but also a good chance for Colm to visit the girls in their homes.

Colm, however, was not so sure about this. These were Protestants, and he was clearly uncomfortable with the idea of visiting them. Colm was the Catholic counterpart of Rob Ross, and he was as nervous around Prods as Rob was around RCs. To build himself up for the meeting, and maybe to delay it, Colm drove me past the little school where he taught, a "wee country school," a century-old building with outdoor toilets and a coal pile in the back. He talked about Bronagh, his girlfriend, and worried out loud about his responsibilities in America. Who would take care of *him* when he got homesick for Bronagh, he wanted to know.

The Montgomery family was waiting for us: fifteen-year-old Susan, her younger brother and sister, and her parents. Her father was a distinguished-looking man, a doctor dressed that Saturday morning in immaculately pressed gray flannels and a blue jacket. Her mother wore a trim leisure suit. Susan, a pretty girl with dark, curly hair, was in the midst of O-levels and anxious to get back to her studies. Nevertheless, tea and biscuits were brought out, and we all did our best to make polite conversation. I could feel Colm twitching on the sofa next to me. This was enemy territory.

"We can't stay long," Colm announced, and in a short time he was maneuvering his little Ford past the Montgomerys' expensive European car. The Montgomerys were lined up at the door, waving. We waved back.

Colm was clearly relieved to be out of there. Now he had only to find the Hunters' farm and leave me, and he was free. "I probably shouldn't say this," he said, "but I would have known they were Protestants as soon as we walked in."

"I probably shouldn't say this either," I said, "but I agree with you."

By that time I had developed a few stereotypes of my own: Protestants, like their hedges, are straight and formal.

The only thing I knew about Sam Hunter was that he was rich, a highly successful businessman who also owned some of the best farmland around Lewistown. I expected velvety green lawns, immaculately groomed shrubbery, a couple of marble lions crouched by the driveway. Colm pulled up in front of an ordinary-looking working farm and checked his directions. "This is it," he announced.

"Can't be," I said. "Look at the hedges." They sprawled every which way. No marble lions by the door; only a clutter of muddy wellies.

A young woman opened the door and waved. "Come on

in," she called. It better have been the right place; Colm was already backing out of the yard. I hung up my coat in the hallway and went into the kitchen. Six people were eating at the kitchen table. A sandy-haired man grinned up at me over a plate of stew. "I have a blacksmith coming this afternoon," he said. "We didn't have time to wait for you." He waved me to an empty place. The young woman set a steaming plate in front of me.

Between mouthfuls we talked about the farmer's thoroughbreds and his cows, sheep, chickens, turkeys. There was another helping of stew followed by apple tart with cream fresh from the cow that morning. But I still didn't know anybody's name.

So we went around the table and introductions were made: Sam and his two sons, his two daughters Jane and Charlotte, who had let me in, and Trav, Charlotte's boyfriend visiting from Belfast for the weekend. Martha, Sam's wife, was away at a horse show; her absence may have accounted for some of the informality.

Jane, a broad-shouldered, rather stocky girl, was dressed in jeans and a baggy sweatshirt and dainty pink satin ballet slippers. You couldn't help noticing those shoes.

"Are you a dancer?" I asked her.

"I want to be," she said. "I've applied to school in London."

Looking at Jane's husky frame, I would not have thought she was dancer's material. But she was one of the few teenagers I met in Northern Ireland who had a dream. Maybe it's easier to be a dreamer in that depressed country when your father is wealthy.

Sam pulled on a ratty pullover, squared a battered cloth cap above his eyebrows, and went out with his sons to find the blacksmith.

"Well, now you've met the wee scruffy man," Charlotte said and poured the rest of us another cup of tea.

Charlotte and Trav are recent Queen's University graduates. She claimed that university students, Protestants and Catholics, are fairly open-minded and mingle freely—probably like those I met at the agricultural college. But later when they go to work and get married and start a family, everyone divides up by tribes. "The older they get, the more they stay apart, with their own."

Trav grew up in a farming village in the Mourne Mountains, near the border of the Republic. Like many others, he worries about what would happen if the Nationalists won out—if there were enough Catholic votes to bring about a unification of North and South. "They'd take over our farms," Trav said. "That would be the end of it." It seemed an irrational fear to me, but perhaps it is not; Trav's ancestors probably took that farm away from Catholics during the plantation.

"Trav thought I was a wee Fenian when he first met me," Charlotte teased. "Didn't you?"

"I did."

Trav said he had never been beaten up by Catholics, but then he wouldn't be foolish enough to stroll someplace like the Falls Road. On the other hand, he *had* been beaten up by Unionist hoods. "Once in Belfast some guys grabbed me shouting, 'Is Ian Paisley the greatest man in the world?' and I yelled 'Yes!' even though I don't think he is, far from it, but I guess I wasn't enthusiastic enough and they beat me up."

(There have been some incidents like that, of one side attacking members of their own tribe, here in Lewistown, too. A director of the youth center at times has had to help Catholic boys beaten by other Catholics for going to the youth center, and take care of Protestants who had been attacked by Protestants for the same reason. Youth centers tend to become the turf of one side or the other despite efforts to keep them neutral.)

Driving back to town in Trav's car, we stopped by the farm where Sam kept his racehorses. When he saw us coming, the "wee scruffy man" swept off his old cloth cap in a courtly bow. I liked him. There was nothing stuffy about him, nothing stiff or pretentious. He had a sense of humor.

"You've got to do something about those hedges, Sam," I said, straight-faced. "I thought for a minute this was a Catholic farm."

Patsy Rafferty Rafferty

Patsy Rafferty married a man named Rafferty, thus acquiring a double name. People with double names, she said, are able to cure the mumps. A person born after the death of the father or, even better, the seventh son of a seventh son, have amazing curative powers. Sometimes the seventh son of a seventh son is even given the name of "Doctor." "They laugh at us in the city," Patsy said. "But it *works*!"

A dozen women, all graduates of St. Mary's Convent School, were getting together at a restaurant a few miles from Lewistown for their annual dinner. They invited me to come along.

But first Patsy and I stopped by a local club to take a look at the *feis* (pronounced FESH), a festival of Irish culture, the kind of things children learn in the Gaeltacht. The feis had been going on for several days, hour after hour of dramatic monologues and recitations (one judge had to listen to ninety-two little girls all recite the same poem in Irish—and pick a winner); performances on piano, tin whistle, piano accordion, button accordion, and violin; and Irish dancing. We went for the dancing.

The girls competing in the seedy auditorium to a weary but loyal audience of parents wore short, flared dresses in bright colors, richly appliqued and embroidered; the lone boy wore a kilt and a jacket. The first dance was a jig, with heavily accented stomps, skips, and jumps. The contestants broke to change shoes, exchanging their clunky jig shoes for thin slippers for the reel, a light, graceful dance. It was like "school figures" in Olympic ice skating, each dancer in turn performing certain required steps. A judge seated on a high chair in the center aisle decided the winner. I was partial to a willowy, slim-legged girl in a white costume and tights; most of the other girls were short and stocky with legs like fire hydrants, but it was one of them who danced off with the prize.

As soon as she could decently pull me away from the feis—for her this was no novelty—Patsy Rafferty Rafferty hustled me off to the dinner. The "girls" of St. Mary's, now in their forties, had reserved a long table, put me at the head of it since I was the guest, and ordered enormous meals. They talked about their children and their husbands—except for a tall, handsome woman in an expensive, red cashmere suit and a chic hairdo, the only stylish woman in the group. One of the women whispered to me that the well-dressed woman was Kathleen, a widow, poor thing; her Tom had up and died when her wee one was only a year old, and her with five older ones to look after. Kathleen didn't look like a "poor thing" to me; she looked in better shape than most of her classmates.

It was about 9:30 when we finished eating and everyone agreed it was time to go. At 10:30 somebody mentioned it again, but no one moved. At 11:30 the subject came up once more. Reluctantly, around midnight the group broke up.

On the way back to town I mentioned the woman in the red suit. "Kathleen has bloomed since Tom died," Patsy said. "He was an alcoholic. Her life was a living hell. But he had made some shrewd investments, so she's all right. And now she's free. Some of the other ones at that table aren't. You probably know that drink is a terrible problem here."

Flashlights appeared on the road ahead, and we were stopped for a police check. Patsy got nervous as she fumbled for her driver's license. "Where ya goin', dear?" the policeman asked. She told him. He handed back the license and waved us on.

"I hate to be called 'dear,' " she sputtered. "I always want to say, 'I'm not your *dear*.' " We joked about calling *him* dear, or luv, or duckie, but neither of us was cheeky enough for that.

It was 1:00 A.M. when I finally got to my room and found the note stuck under my door. "I'll pick you up at 8:00 A.M. for mass at the army base." Signed, "Paul."

Sunday Morning

British troops were first called into Northern Ireland in 1969, when the Royal Ulster Constabulary was no longer able to contain the rioting in Londonderry and Belfast. The soldiers had arrived during the height and the heat of the marching season, as thousands of Orangemen converged on Derry from all over the province. Most people wanted the parade to be stopped, but officials refused. When the police lost control of the situation, the military seemed to be the only way to restore order. A newspaper of that time reported that the British army "was greeted with profound relief on the Catholic side. . . . But the troops were met with a cold and hostile reaction from many on the Protestant side."

Times have changed. The Catholics have come to hate the British and want them out of Northern Ireland. The troops stay because the Protestants insist that the British government maintain a "military presence" in Northern Ireland.

Protestants are afraid that if the troops are withdrawn, there will be a civil war, that Catholics from the Republic will join forces with Catholics from the North and overrun them.

Meanwhile, the army is indeed a presence, noticeable in every town, on the main streets and major intersections of Belfast, out on the highways. And a number of them are garrisoned in Lewistown. Some of these men are Catholic, or they married Catholic women when they were first greeted as saviors in 1969. Father Paul, despite the disapproval of his parishioners, says mass in the base chapel every Sunday morning for military families who would not feel comfortable—or safe—coming into town to church.

"It would be so easy," Paul said matter-of-factly, "for somebody to rig my car, put a time bomb in the boot or the engine. I never lock it, and I never check it. I could simply drive in here some Sunday morning and blow us all to Kingdom Come."

I wished he hadn't said that. I waited for him in his possibly booby-trapped car in the driveway outside the guard's station, also a vulnerable place to be. A young soldier with pink cheeks stood sleepy-eyed at the gate. It seemed to me that the priest had been inside getting our passes for an unusually long time. An unnecessarily long time. At last he came out, and we drove on to the chapel.

Only a handful of people showed up. The woman who was to read the Old Testament lesson and the psalm was not there. Father Paul asked if I'd fill in. I stood at the lectern and read the lesson from the Book of Exodus, Moses and his people wandering in the wilderness. Mass went smoothly. Father Paul eliminated any sexist references he encountered in the service, by changing them ("man" to "human") or omitting them.

This surprised me. Feminism seems not to exist in Northern Ireland, so far as I could tell; I heard about one crusty old priest who refuses to allow women any role whatsoever in his parish. "The church is a failure if it has to rely on the help of women," the old man reportedly told his curates.

When mass was over I talked with the wife of a British soldier. She was originally from Belfast, but she never goes there any more, even though her family still lives there. It was better when her husband was stationed in another country; then she could go to visit her family freely. Her husband carries a gun wherever they go, for his own protection and his family's. She sends her children to the parish school and worries about their safety.

"I hated to come back to Northern Ireland, to the tension and violence," she said. "I thought about staying in England with the children while my husband was in Northern Ireland for this tour of duty. But then I thought, what if something happens to him? I wanted the children and me to be with him for as much time as we have."

He would be rotated out in a few months. Meanwhile, all she could do was pray.

The sadness of this army wife's situation contrasted sharply with the mood in the British Officers' Mess where Father Paul and I stopped for a cup of tea before driving back to Lewistown. The officers were recuperating from an all-night party with a "Roaring 20s" theme. Men were dismantling a huge tent out on the soggy lawn. The long dining room where we sipped our tea was under the benign gaze of portraits of the Queen Mother as a young girl and an assortment of proper English princesses. A stuffed, regimental boar's head hung above the door. A pair of ivory tusks and an elephant's foot, mementoes of colonial days, ornamented the foyer. Polite young men with very short hair moved quietly about, addressing Father Paul as "sir," causing him to grimace.

"It used to be," Paul said as we headed toward the gate, "that people came here to picnic on the grass. It was like a public park. Not any more. The soldiers are like prisoners here."

"Did I mention that you're going to the Presbyterian church at half eleven? Mr. Creighton, the minister, wants you to say a few words to the congregation."

No, he hadn't mentioned that. "Say a few words to the congregation about *what*?"

Father Paul breezily waved off my question. "You'll sort it out with him. I have to say mass in a country chapel now. I'll drop you at St. Mary's. You can watch the place fill up and then go across the street to the Presbyterians."

St. Mary's is one of four churches on Hill Street. It was 10:45, and the next mass was at eleven. I stood at the back end of the enormous church and watched the crowd grow for the third mass of the morning, ushers bringing more and more people to jam the pews and overflow into the aisles. The priest celebrating mass at the ornate high altar seemed very far away, and the P.A. system scratched and crackled. Somewhere there was an organ and a choir, but they also seemed remote. I preferred the tiny group in the chapel on the army base; so did Father Paul, who dreamed of being transferred some day to a little rural church where he'd know every worshiper in his flock.

As some twelve hundred Catholics packed St. Mary's, I wondered what on earth I was expected to say to the Presbyterians. Then I had an inspiration: I would tell them how important it was for me as an American to have the freedom to "cross sectarian lines," as they say there—to participate first in a Roman Catholic mass and then to join the Presbyterians in their worship of the same God, the same Christ. Feeling better, I slipped out of St. Mary's, crossed the street, passed the Church of Ireland and the Methodist church, all filling with worshipers, and went looking for Mr. Creighton.

He had not yet arrived, but his long black robe was warming by the electric fire. At 11:25, while my palms were growing damp, he bustled in, a portly man with thinning hair. An assistant helped him into his robe as he gave me my instructions—where to sit, what to read, how long to speak.

Then I told him about my inspiration: I would read the same scripture I had read at mass at the base, and then I'd explain to the congregation that it was the same one I read to the Catholics, and from there I'd talk about crossing sectarian lines and—

"You will not," said Mr. Creighton firmly. "You will not even mention that you have been to mass this morning. Many people in this church would not be able to accept that. They would be upset and angry."

That was that. I meekly followed an usher to a high-backed chair facing the congregation. It was a simple church with plain white pews and plain glass windows, New England Puritan in its starkness. A hundred or so people, most of the women in hats, stared at me soberly. I read what I was told to read and said something harmless and inoffensive, explaining why I was there. Then Mr. Creighton made a little speech of welcome and a plea "for the good will of the American people for Northern Ireland during these troubled times." I knew, and they knew, that most Americans support the Irish Catholics.

Mrs. Creighton, the minister's doughty wife, swept the children into a formal group and announced that I was going to tell them all about Sunday Schools in the United States, a subject about which I know nothing. Instead I talked about a book I had written a dozen years ago on American crafts, for which I had interviewed potters, blacksmiths, glassblowers, and so on. I got caught up in my own idea and began to elaborate on the transformation of simple material—clay, iron, sand—into something beautiful by skilled hands with God-given talent.

I sensed that I was talking too much, that the kids were probably not as excited by this subject as I was. So I asked if there was anything they wanted to ask me. A few hands shot up, and I called on a little boy dressed up in a bow tie.

"What's the longest river in the United States?"

I blinked. "The Mississippi."

"What's the biggest lake?" "The highest mountain?" "The tallest building?"

"What's going on?" I wondered. "Do you have a geography exam tomorrow?"

Mrs. Creighton intervened. "You are testing Miss Meyer," she said sternly. "But you have not found her wanting! Now perhaps some of you have *sensible* questions for our visitor."

A girl in a yellow outfit shyly raised her hand. "Miss, have you ever been in an earthquake?"

Class dismissed.

For the next few days I saw a lot of Father Paul, but I saw even more of Rob Ross. On Sunday afternoon we gathered up a carload of Channels of Peace people and drove to the Ulster-American Folk Park. The park is divided into two parts, one the Old World with Irish cottages, thatched roofs, and peat fires, the other the New World with log cabins and quilts. On the way back we discovered that Andrew, a boy with a mischievous grin but not much to say, was subject to carsickness. Then we got stuck in a traffic jam for at least twenty minutes while spectators at a soccer game—they called it a football match—clogged the roads and local police tried ineffectually to untangle the mess. Stops were frequent.

Often Rob and I just sat and talked. He belongs to the Church of Ireland, a tradition that is not as dramatically different from Catholic liturgy as a Presbyterian service is, and he had just been to mass with Father Paul. "How was it?" I asked.

"All right," he said. "It's the first time for me. Me family is shocked that I'm doing all these things."

"First thing you know, you'll be converting," I teased him, but Rob didn't see anything amusing about that.

"Me feelings go much too deep to do anything like that," he said solemnly. The whole idea of confession, of going into that box and telling a priest about your sins, and being given prayers to say as punishment—well, that was too much.

The subject changed, but after a while Rob came back to it. "Have you noticed," he asked me, "that Father Paul always refers to Protestants as 'non-Catholics'? How would he like it if we called Catholics 'non-Protestants'?"

"Let's try it the next time we see him," I suggested, "and find out."

"Where are you having your tea?" Rob asked. In Northern Ireland country people refer to the evening meal as "tea," no matter how substantial it is—or how late. I planned to eat in the hotel dining room, since there were no restaurants nearby, and Rob wondered if he could come too—his mum wasn't at home, and he'd be on his own.

I was pleased to have his company, but I was glad for another reason: it was a chance to repay his generosity. For the past couple of days Rob had insisted on paying my way everywhere we went—small amounts, a pound for admission to the Folk Park, a few pence for a soda in a pub, but it added up. I wanted to do something in return, and so I took the waitress aside and told her to put the check on my hotel bill.

Rob ordered a steak (well done; he believes a piece of beef needs to be cooked for at least an hour to be edible) with plenty of chips (french fries), but skip the vegetables, please. He decided a glass of wine might go well with it and then topped it off with a large dessert of some kind buried under a cloud of whipped cream. My meal was similar, although I was trying to cut down on desserts. As we were finishing, I was called to the telephone; when I came back there was no sign of the check, and I assumed it had been put on my account. Later I found out that it had not, and that Rob had paid for the whole meal—his and mine. It must have taken a big chunk of his paycheck.

I didn't know what to do, so I went to Father Paul. "He can't afford to do this," I said. "He's got a part-time job, he earns hardly any money, he's going to America next month and needs every cent he can get his hands on. I can't let him pay for that meal. What do I do now?"

"Let it go," the priest said. "Do you realize what it meant for him to be able to pay your way—a woman, a writer, an American? He bought much more than a meal with that money. He bought himself a big helping of self-esteem. Let him enjoy it."

So I did the only thing possible—thanked Rob and enjoyed his beaming smile.

VII

BLUE RIVER, USA: THE AMERICAN CONNECTION

Irish Night

Two months after I left Lewistown, a month after I got home, I caught up again with the Channels of Peace group in an American city I've renamed Blue River. I wanted to see how they were faring. They were all sunburned and proud of it—for some that was *the* main objective of the trip. There was Colm Gillespie in white shorts, red thighs, red knees, red nose, and a tee shirt with Channels of Peace/Blue River printed on it. He was standing on a high-school stage with a microphone in his hand, acting as MC for "Irish Night." It was the group's last weekend in Blue River, and Irish Night was the traditional farewell from the Ulster students to their host families and others who had been working on the project.

When I met the group in Lewistown at the end of May, everyone was in a state of anxiety: letters had not yet arrived from Blue River to tell them about the families with whom they would stay and to introduce their American counterparts. At that time the sixteen Catholic and Protestant boys and girls were getting together regularly to work out plans for Irish Night. It was their first joint project, a way for the two sides to start learning to cooperate. The Catholic girls, for instance, were teaching the Protestant girls the fundamentals of Irish dancing, the kind of thing I had seen at the feis.

Now in Blue River eight barefoot girls in shorts and Channels of Peace tee shirts bounded onto the high-school stage and executed the sprightly steps of a reel. The next act was a tin whistle played by Andrew, the boy who got sick in my backseat. A couple of girls sang duets. Somebody sat down at the piano and stumbled through a familiar recital piece by Beethoven. More singing. Colm came out and did a stand-up comedy routine, told a few flat jokes, and with great emotion recited a few sentimental poems from his childhood. I was seated between the grandmothers of one of the host teenagers, and I was careful not to look anywhere but straight ahead during a series of "impressions" done by a totally uninhibited boy named Matt. They were pretty bad, awfully tasteless, but Matt's American friends in the audience thought they were hysterically funny.

When I first began meeting Channels of Peace leaders and students in Northern Ireland, they told me gleefully about the meetings they had in which they were instructed *never* to use certain words and expressions around their American hosts, for fear of shocking or offending them.

Never say "I'm dying for a fag" when you want a cigarette.

Never say "I need a rubber" when you want an eraser.

There were no cultural problems with Matt's jokes. His language was universally bad.

The evening ended with everybody singing Irish songs, led by Colm. We started off with "Cockles and Mussels" ("In

Dublin's fair city. . . ."). Next came "It's a Long Way to Tipperary" (another town in the Republic), "When Irish Eyes Are Smiling," and "Hail, Glorious St. Patrick." None of them were songs an Ulster Protestant would pick. It was plainly Colm's idea of Irish Night.

Susan and Jane

Jane, the daughter of the "wee scruffy man" in the old cloth cap, and Susan, the daughter of the man in the creased flannel trousers, met me the next morning. Susan's host family had gone out: Esther and Mac Gardiner, their fifteen-year-old daughter Linda and eight-year-old Lisa. We sat in the Gardiners' air-conditioner-chilled living room. Susan was the orderly, perfectly groomed, beautifully mannered girl that I remembered. Jane showed up in shorts and baggy tee shirt and told me that she had been accepted in a ballet school in London. Susan brought a box of cookies from the kitchen which Jane attacked as though she hadn't eaten since yesterday and then asked Susan to hide them from her.

I asked how they liked it here, in Blue River, in America.

"I'm thinking about coming back to go to university," Susan said. "I want to study law, and if I do that in Northern Ireland then the only place I can practice is in the U.K. And I don't want to stay there. This would be better.

"But if I lived in America, I'd try to stick to an Irish diet," she said, munching a chocolate chip cookie. "It's much healthier."

"An Irish diet is healthier than an American diet?" I remembered all those potatoes, the overcooked meat and vegetables, the absence of salads and the lack of fresh fruit.

"Everything here is sweet," she explained. "There's sugar in cereal, in everything. We don't eat like that."

"How are you getting along with Linda and the Gardiners?"

"It's terrible the way Linda talks to her mother," Susan said. "She expects her mother to do everything for her, buy her whatever she wants, take her wherever she wants to go. And Lisa whines all the time. My sister is a much nicer child to be around. These children don't seem to respect their parents."

"Debbie's not like that," Jane said, referring to her host family. "She and her mother get along just fine. They talk about *everything*. Debbie tells her mother about her boyfriends. We never talk about anything like that with our parents. We're much more formal than people here."

"I'm really getting sick of some of Linda's friends," Susan said. "They deliberately shut me out. They talk *around* me."

How were they feeling after almost a month with Channels of Peace?

Annoyed, they said. Irritated. Sick and tired of Colm and his aggressive, know-it-all attitude.

Aggressive, know-it-all attitude? My impression of Colm back in Lewistown was that he was quiet, shy, maybe a little insecure. But it was true that on the high-school stage last evening he had not been at all quiet and shy. He not only ran the show but, in fact, nearly overwhelmed it.

"He keeps bringing up issues we've never even *heard* of," Jane complained.

"I was probably not really a good person to send on this trip," Susan said. "I've never been angry or bitter towards Catholics. The leaders asked us if we felt angry or bitter, and I had to say I never have."

"But did you hear what that girl Brenda said?" Jane demanded. "She said we took away their land! Who is she to say such a thing?"

"Who's Brenda?" I asked.

"A Catholic girl," Susan explained. "And she keeps saying that the Protestants took away the Catholics' farms, which isn't true at all. The Scottish people were sent over to improve the use of the land. And they did it very well, too!"

I could scarcely believe that Susan knew nothing about the plantation, had never heard of the Penal Laws, was ignorant of the harsh penalties historically applied to Catholics. I knew, though, that Catholics and Protestants aren't taught the same kind of history, and their comments seemed to bear that out.

"I got tired of hearing it," Jane said. "I just told Brenda that if my ancestors actually did take her ancestors' land, don't blame it on me. It's not my fault."

But that is what the problem of Northern Ireland is all about: people doomed by history to carry on their ancestors' hatreds.

Colm is homesick, they said. He calls his girlfriend back in Lewistown and runs up huge phone bills. They laughed at his ridiculous tee shirts, but they thought one of them was appropriate. It said: PEOPLE WHO THINK THEY KNOW IT ALL ANNOY THOSE OF US WHO DO.

"Has this experience changed anything for you?" I asked.

Susan and Jane looked at each other. "Not really," they agreed. Then they began discussing between themselves what might be different when they returned to Lewistown. "We already had Catholic friends at home," Susan said. "But as for those from this program. . . ." She didn't finish the sentence.

Colm Gillespie and Lucy Knight

It was hard to find a place to take Colm for lunch; he hated American food. American mayonnaise was too spicy for him. We drove past the Italian restaurant I wanted to go to because

Colm wouldn't eat Italian food and ended up at a beef restaurant where he ordered a well-done hamburger.

Colm was seething with frustration. Nothing about the trip had worked out as he expected. "This is the one chance we might ever have to get down to real issues," he complained, "and no one wants to do it. Tina, the breakthrough leader, doesn't know anything at all about Northern Ireland, and so she wants to talk about faith. *Faith* isn't the issue. I keep trying to tell them that, but no one will listen. *Politics* is the issue."

The sixteen kids from Northern Ireland were in Blue River for a month, and their hosts had gone all out to make them feel at home, to keep them entertained—but not to challenge them. One day they were invited to someone's luxurious riverside home; four powerboats had been rounded up, and the Ulster boys and girls were towed up and down on inner tubes, boards, and—the few who had gotten the hang of it—water skis. They had been taken on trips to the state capital and to amusement parks and other tourist attractions. They had been fed hamburgers, hot dogs, and pizza.

And once a week they had been brought together for a two-hour "breakthrough" session, led by a psychologist skilled in getting people to open up and say what they really thought and felt. But, according to Colm, she didn't know enough about Northern Ireland to do the job right. He tried to set her straight.

"It's not a matter of Catholic against Protestant but of Nationalist against Unionist. It has nothing to do with religion! It's all politics. It's more important for the Prods to understand that not all RCs are Republicans or IRA supporters, and the RCs need to understand that not all Prods are Paisleyites who think Catholics ought to be exterminated."

Colm was certain that he was entirely rational, that his arguments were intellectually sound. But Colm's problem, it became clear, was that he didn't know when to shut up. And now nobody would listen to him.

"The truth is, I don't really want to be here," Colm confessed. "I only came because the rector at St. Mary's, Father Donovan, said I must. I miss me girlfriend. As far as I'm concerned, this whole Channels of Peace program is a failure. The money could be much better spent in other ways—like feeding the hungry in Africa. Here it is, the chance of a lifetime for us to get together and say all the things we can't even think of saying at home, and no one will let it happen. Every time we get close to some serious issues, the Prods back off."

Colm described an incident on the bus coming back from their visit to the state capital. One of the boys started singing "God Save the Queen," and nearly everybody joined in, including Catholics who would not normally want to sing a Unionist song. Then they started "The Sash," a song from the Orange Order. "I would have expected the Catholics to resist that one, but they joined in. And one of the Catholic girls wanted the Protestants to teach her the words. But when I started singing a Nationalist song, 'The Man Behind the Wire,' the Prods got very upset." His theory is that Catholics will sing Protestant songs, but not the other way around. He may be right; I don't know his song, but the title alone suggests that it probably wasn't the one to test the theory.

Meanwhile, Colm was reeling from culture shock, and it had to do with more than just spicy mayonnaise. Like many Catholics in Ireland (Father Paul and Bridie McHugh are exceptions) Colm is extremely conservative, and he was horrified by what he saw as the liberalism of American Catholics. He was not accustomed to the idea of saying no to a priest; it didn't occur to him to refuse Father Donovan's request that he accompany a group of teenagers to another country, even when he didn't want to go. He saw it as an order that if refused could cost him his job.

Colm didn't think much of the Protestants he met in America either. He was convinced that they were all out to convert Catholics, because (in his view) American Protestant ministers are paid according to the size of their congregations. If there's not exactly a bounty on the head of every Catholic lured into the Protestant church, it's something close to it.

I did manage to coax Lucy, Colm's Protestant counterpart, to the Italian restaurant. She was not as squeamish as Colm about American food. We ate meatball grinders and wondered how Rob Ross was doing in another part of the country with his group, if he had run into the kind of problems Lucy found.

"Rob seems so young for this kind of job, so unsure of himself," she said. "But he is very well organized. He was completely ready a week ahead of time, and I was still throwing things together the night before."

Lucy is slim and athletic and caught on immediately to waterskiing. In her early twenties, studying in London with another year to her degree, she went home to Lewistown at the end of the term in May and was immediately recruited to go to America as a counselor with Channels of Peace. An easygoing sort, she was not nearly as critical of Colm as he was of her. She said he had been moping ever since he arrived, dithering over his girlfriend at home, refusing to go out socializing with the other counselors.

"He says he wouldn't have a good time if he goes out with us. He wouldn't be able to think of anything but her. And I told him if he went with us then he wouldn't be thinking of her every minute. Apparently he's deeply in love."

Lucy understood Colm's frustration without really understanding the source of it. She saw Colm as a basically authoritarian person used to teaching primary-age children who don't talk back, a person who knows nothing about teenagers. "Colm thinks these kids have political views that need to be brought up and discussed. I don't believe that," Lucy said. "They've absorbed their parents' views and simplified them. But that doesn't mean they know enough to take part in a political discussion."

In Lucy's family her parents hold strong anti-Catholic prejudices, she said, but she and her sisters are far more moderate. That does not mean she would ever consider entering into a mixed marriage, although there is one in her family: an aunt and uncle locked her cousin in his room when he said he wanted to marry a Catholic girl, but the girl converted, they got married, and now she celebrates the Twelfth of July even more enthusiastically than the rest of the family.

"It's funny," Lucy said. "One of my roommates in London is Catholic, several of my friends there are Catholic, we get into screaming matches over politics and religion. In England, like here in America, it doesn't matter what you are. But at home it matters. You *have* to know what somebody's religion is. You have to know who you're talking to."

Colm showed up at the evaluation meeting for Blue River's Channels of Peace program in his usual shorts and shrunken tee shirt and made one last stand at getting through to the American planning committee and Lucy. He was dogged and aggressive. He insisted again that the main issues were political, not religious. He hammered on the idea that there weren't enough breakthrough sessions—that one a day would be more like it, not one a week. He said that for most of the teenagers it had been nothing more than a holiday. He repeated stubbornly that Protestants didn't want to get into politics. He badgered Lucy until finally someone told him to shut up.

I stopped Colm as he was leaving. He looked disconsolate and haggard. I told him I thought he was basically right on many points, but he was wrong in hammering on it.

That evening everyone—Ulster teens, American teens, committee, staff—gathered in a carpeted "conference pit" in a Blue River church. Everybody piled into the pit—except Colm, who sat apart, his arms clamped across his chest. Candles were passed around and lighted. A few Christian songs were sung. Prayers for peace were said. Candles were extinguished and everybody hugged one another and cried a little. A dozen pizzas were trotted out from the church kitchen. Everybody munched them down and hugged some more and talked and laughed.

Everybody except Colm.

VIII

THE REPUBLIC OF IRELAND: POETS, MARTYRS, AND A MILLION EMIGRANTS

"You must go to Donegal," the poet said. "It will heal you."

We had been talking about the Troubles for an hour or so, and I had been talking about the Troubles, or some aspect of life in Northern Ireland, almost nonstop for three weeks. I was tired, beginning to fray around the edges. Denis, the poet, could see that. Donegal was his prescription. Fair weather was predicted, and if I were lucky I would have a fine day or two.

And so I drove across the border, out of Northern Ireland and into a different country. Donegal really *is* a different country, part of the Republic of Ireland, one of the three counties of Ulster, which, along with Cavan and Monaghan to the south, was sliced off at the time of the partition. Donegal is wild, rugged, beautiful country but very poor, its standard of living far below that of Northern Ireland next door. That was obvious immediately, simply by the condition of the roads. Streets and highways in Northern Ireland are generally well maintained, but the roads of Donegal—and many other parts of the Republic—were falling into disrepair, potholed and crumbling.

Crossing the border also meant changing to a different currency system and a different economy. Northern Ireland uses British currency, in pounds and pence that correspond to dollars and cents; the Republic has its own currency, the Irish pound or *punt*, but it looks different and is worth less. Because of the difference between the two economies, I could spend my British money in the Republic, but no one in Northern Ireland would accept pounds or pence from the South.

Then there was the matter of the road signs. Donegal is the heart of the Gaeltacht, one of the few remaining parts of Ireland where Irish is still spoken. The signposts—small, white-painted, wooden signs with faded black lettering—are set right at the crossroads, with no advance warning. And most of the place names are in Irish. Although sometimes there was a faint similarity between the Irish names and their English equivalents, a few of the same consonants with a string of vowels in between, I generally could not read the names of the towns on the signposts, and so I didn't know where I was. It didn't matter. All I wanted to do was follow the seacoast, not really caring where I was going or when I got there, as long as I was within sight of the sea.

That evening I stopped in a little village with a small hotel that served excellent salmon. A fine mist had settled in, and most of the local people turned up to listen to three musicians playing traditional Irish music in the pub. They ordered tall mugs of mahogany-colored stout with inches of foam on top and talked to one another in a language I didn't understand. They ignored me, an outsider, pretending I wasn't there. Denis the poet had not warned me about that.

The conversation with Denis and the brooding landscape served as reminders that Ireland is traditionally a land of poets and writers. William Butler Yeats, the great lyric poet who died in 1939, and novelist James Joyce, probably our century's most significant writer in the English language, who died two years later, were both well acquainted with the Troubles of their time. Yeats wrote not only of the beauty of the countryside, but of the ugliness of violence. The tradition is kept alive today by poets like Seamus Heaney, born the year Yeats died, who writes in contemporary images: "One morning early I met armoured cars/In convoy, warbling along on powerful tyres,/All camouflaged with broken alder branches,/And headphoned soldiers standing up in turrets . . . O charioteers, above your dormant guns. . . ."

The next day I continued my wandering, turning away from the wild Atlantic coast and heading east across the desolate, rock-strewn hills. By noon I realized I was going in circles. I was looking for Letterkenny, and although I could figure out the name in Irish, I never seemed to get any closer to it. A couple of times I stopped to ask directions, first from a young farm boy and then from an old farmer. Each was going somewhere and needed a lift. Each pointed the way and disappeared, and I realized each had taken me by the route that passed near his destination but got me no closer to mine.

Eventually I found my way out of the maze of pretty country roads, stark landscapes, and vast peatbogs and crossed the border back into Northern Ireland. The feeling of sadness enveloped me again.

Of the six weeks I was in Ireland, seven days were spent in the Republic: enroute to Belfast via Dublin; a scant twenty-four hours in Donegal; at the end on my way to Shannon Airport. It was in the Republic of Ireland that I discovered a sense of the history of the island as a whole, not just a fragment broken off for political reasons.

I have written in earlier chapters of historical events leading up to the partition, particularly the arrival of various groups that continue to play out their separate roles. But just as important to the history of Ireland as the successive arrivals are the *departures*. Ireland's biggest, most important export, from all political divisions of the island, is its people. Among the first to leave were the Scottish Presbyterians, called Scotch-Irish when they arrived in America in the eighteenth century. The next great emigration occurred in the middle of the nineteenth century, the result of the potato famine. A number of events led up to that.

Toward the end of the eighteenth century an Anglican named Theobald Wolfe Tone, who was sympathetic to the plight of both Presbyterians and Catholics oppressed by the English, formed the Society of United Irishmen, a radical organization committed to "principles of civil, political, and religious liberty." The goal of the United Irishmen was to persuade the parliaments of Britain and Dublin to end the Penal Laws, enacted a century earlier to prevent "Protestants intermarrying with Papists" and "Popish Priests from coming into this Kingdom," and to make it impossible for Catholics to buy land, teach school, or enjoy many other civil liberties.

The French Revolution inspired Wolfe Tone to plan an uprising. He counted on the French to help the Irish with their rebellion; that help never came. In 1798 he and his supporters lost the battle, Wolfe Tone was captured, and he cut his own throat. He became one of the early patriots.

The British were as determined as ever to exert full control over the rebellious Irish. They abolished the Parliament in Dublin and passed the Act of Union in 1800 to unite Ireland and Britain. A new flag, called the Union Jack, combined three crosses symbolizing the union of Scotland, Ireland, and England in the United Kingdom of Great Britain. Over the next few decades there were more attempts to press the cause for Catholic rights, and a few concessions were won. Things seemed to be getting better. But then disaster struck Ireland.

In the nineteenth century Irish peasants produced two crops: wheat and other grain were paid to the English landlord as rent and then exported to England; the second crop was potatoes. Potatoes were easy to grow; a few acres were enough to feed a peasant's family and his animals. But beginning in 1845 and for several years after that, a blight destroyed the potato crop. The peasants had a choice: they could continue to send the grain crops to their landlords and starve, or they could eat the grain themselves and be evicted from their land for failure to pay the rent.

There was plenty of food, but the Irish peasants were not allowed to eat it. For too long the British remained indifferent, doing nothing about the situation. When they did act, it was too late. A million people died in the potato famine, and over a million more left Ireland. Some people believe that the Irish were deliberately allowed to starve to get rid of troublesome peasants who were no longer needed as the price of grain dropped and many landlords turned their wheat fields into pastures and meadows.

Whether it was deliberate or not, the effects were the same: a quarter of the population of Ireland died and another quarter left. The Irish peasants were not allowed to go to England, although they were British citizens. Instead they sailed to the United States or to Canada in ships that became floating coffins for thousands who died at sea. Many who stayed behind kept alive the memory of those times. The memories became myths that still feed their hatred of the British.

About 1858, a revolutionary organization called the Fenian Society was formed in Ireland and in the United States, taking its name from a military group that served the high kings of Ireland in the third century. ("Fenian" became a derogatory name for a Catholic.) The Fenians' goal was to get the English out of Ireland. Sometimes called the Irish Republican Brotherhood, they staged more risings—and met with more failures.

One of the issues that kept the Irish up in arms was the land question. Seventy percent of Ireland was farmland, but in 1870 only 3 percent of the people were landowners. Most of those were descended from Scottish and English Protestants who had taken land away from the Catholics; the Catholics were only tenant farmers. Eventually competition from America forced prices down and Protestant landlords sold off their land; by 1916, 64 percent of the population owned land.

British prime minister William Gladstone tried to improve relations with the Irish by making another change. He *disestablished* the Church of Ireland, declaring that the Protestant CofI was no longer the official religion of Ireland and would no longer be supported by public money—money paid in taxes by the Roman Catholic majority.

But still the Irish weren't satisfied. Now they wanted Home Rule: an Irish Parliament in Dublin to be in charge of Irish affairs. A Protestant named Charles Stewart Parnell was chosen leader of the Home Rule Party. But Parnell wasn't satisfied with home rule only; he wanted complete independence for Ireland.

Despite laws that helped to protect tenant farmers against their landlords, the farmers were still unhappy. Parnell advised tenants evicted from their farms to refuse to deal with both the landlord and the new tenant who had been hired at a lower wage, "leaving him severely alone." Shunning can be effective punishment. When a landlord's agent named Charles Boycott was given this treatment, the English language gained a new word: *boycott*.

Gladstone, seeing that nothing else would work, decided to support Home Rule. But the Unionists—Protestants who were loyal to England—opposed Gladstone. They went to Conservative leader Randolph Churchill, the father of Winston Churchill, to help them stop Home Rule. Churchill's slogan was "Ulster will fight. Ulster will be right!" His idea was to enlist the aid of the Orange Order to unite the Protestants in Ulster against Home Rule. He called this "playing the Orange Card."

Playing the Orange Card kept alive hatred and discrimination against Catholics. The issue of Home Rule went on for years. In 1913 the Ulster Volunteer Force was formed to stop Home Rule by force, if necessary.

The fears that started the Troubles brewing over seventy years ago are the same fears that keep the Troubles brewing today. Two thirds of the population of Ulster is Protestant; they own most of the land and most of the businesses. In the Republic of Ireland, Protestants are a tiny minority. If Ireland were united into one country, the Roman Catholics would outnumber the Protestants and outvote them. Protestants are afraid the Catholic church would then interfere in the way their children are educated, make divorce illegal throughout the country, and eliminate other rights. A referendum to allow divorce in the Republic, where it is prohibited by the constitution, was defeated by a huge majority in June 1986. "Home Rule is Rome rule," Unionists say.

During World War I, the Unionists, loyal to England and the Crown, sent 35,000 members of the Ulster Volunteer Force to fight on the side of the British Army. Thousands of them died. When the war ended, the grateful British could not then turn against the majority of the people of Ulster and allow them to become part of the Republic against their will.

Meanwhile, Irish nationalism was on the rise. The Nationalists formed the Gaelic Athletic Association in 1884 to revive ancient Celtic sports like Gaelic football and hurling. A few years later the Gaelic League was founded to stimulate the use of the Irish language and to make it the official national language. (Today Irish and English are both official languages in the Republic; the Irish language has no status in Northern Ireland.) Sinn Fein—meaning *Ourselves Alone* and pronounced SHIN FAYN—was founded as a new political party to work for complete independence for Ireland by peaceful means.

Strikes and the threat of civil war persisted for decades. Along came another leader, a schoolteacher and poet named Patrick Pearse, who, inspired by the example of Wolfe Tone more than a century before, joined the Irish Republican Brotherhood and called for another rising. He and his followers planned to take over Dublin on Easter 1916. As usual everything went wrong. After a week of bloody street fighting the rebel leaders surrendered, and Pearse and fourteen others were executed by a firing squad. Yeats wrote in his poem "Easter 1916," "Too long a sacrifice/Can make a stone of the heart."

After the Easter Rising, Sinn Fein gained support and the Irish Republican Army (IRA) was formed. In 1919 the IRA launched terrorist attacks on British police and soldiers, beginning the War of Independence. There seemed to be only one way to stop the war; in 1920 the Government of Ireland Act was passed, dividing Ireland into two countries, the twenty-six counties of the South to be called the Irish Free State, and the six counties of Northern Ireland, each country to have Home Rule. At this point Northern Ireland began its separate history.

This satisfied the Unionists, but the Nationalists still demanded independence. Assassinations, bombings, and fighting continued between those who favored the peace treaty and those who opposed it. This hopeless split resulted in a civil war that ended in 1923 with defeat for those who did not want Ireland to be partitioned. One of the defeated leaders was Eamon de Valera, the American-born son of an Irish mother and a Spanish father, who eventually rose to become president of the Irish Free State.

Renamed Eire in 1937, the country stayed neutral during World War II while Northern Ireland fought on the side of the British, and the IRA, outlawed in 1936, collaborated with the Germans. After the war, Eire changed its name again, this time to the Republic of Ireland.

The Nationalists of Northern Ireland still yearn for a united Ireland, most of them through peaceful means. But the IRA in the North, called the Provisional IRA or "Provos," commits acts of terror almost daily, believing that terrorism is the only way to rid Northern Ireland of the British presence so that the island can be united.

Meanwhile the Unionists vow "No surrender!" and "Not an inch!"—insisting that they will never consent to separate from the United Kingdom and become part of the Republic of Ireland. They have their own paramilitary and terrorist organizations to match the IRA, act for bloody act.

In 1981 Provisional IRA men imprisoned in the Maze Prison H-Block in Northern Ireland demanded to be treated as political prisoners, to be allowed to wear their own clothes instead of prison garb. When their demands were refused, they went on a hunger strike, a very old form of protest. Ten of the men starved themselves to death; the most famous was Bobby Sands.

Not all Catholics in Northern Ireland are Republicans or want to become part of the Republic of Ireland. As part of the U.K., they benefit from social services like free education and free medical care. Even with massive unemployment, Northern Ireland is considerably better off economically than the South, and so are the people who live there. But the

Catholics of the North are not willing to trade off discrimination and powerlessness as the price to pay for better economic conditions.

Nobody seems to know what to do about it. "The problem is that we don't know what the problem is," someone told me. Another said, "The problem is that there is no solution." A familiar Belfast expression is, "If you think you're not confused you just don't know what's going on."

Northern Ireland was, for me, a depressed and depressing place. There seems to be a kind of national neurosis that grips everybody, whether they are aware of it or not. The basis of that neurosis is the fear of change. Northern Ireland is an extremely conservative country where change—any kind of change—is threatening. Compromise, the idea that one gives up something in order to get something else, represents change. Ulster focuses on what must be given up, not on what might be gained.

For example, one obvious place to start bringing people together so that they can understand one another is in the schools. Some experts believe that separating children into camps when they're very young might be a major cause of the conflict. Children who have contact with the "other side" are less likely to grow up with blind hatreds—and the logical place to get that contact is in school. The Catholic Church, however, is obstinately opposed to integrated education.

I asked Father Paul his opinion. This priest struck me as an open-minded man; he had edited the words of the mass to eliminate sexist references and allowed non-Catholics to receive communion if they wished. But he was evasive on the subject of integrated education. "I would have to rethink my whole philosophy of parochial education," he hedged, suggesting that the only way to become a good Catholic is to attend Catholic schools.

On the other side, Protestants cling tightly to what they've got, threatened by the idea that any gain in housing, jobs, or political power for Catholics is an unacceptable loss for them. The Anglo-Irish agreement signed in November of 1985 is a complicated attempt to juggle a number of different aims and desires: the aim of the Republic of Ireland to unite with Northern Ireland; the aim of the Protestants of Northern Ireland to remain part of the U.K.; the desire of the Catholic minority for a way to express its grievances against the political and social system. The agreement is an attempt to end the bloodshed that began in 1969 and has left more than 2,450 people dead and countless others maimed and wounded. To make the agreement more palatable for the Protestant Unionists, the United States offered to send $250 million in aid to the province.

The reaction was predictable: the Unionists hate it. On the Twelfth of July 1986, 3,500 militant Protestants, some masked or wearing military-style uniforms, staged a mock siege of the town where the agreement was signed. And most of the Catholics—with the exception of Provo terrorists—see it as a step forward.

Northern Ireland seems no more able to escape its hopelessness than it can its wretched weather. When I crossed the border after twenty-four hours in Donegal, I had three more weeks to go. I wondered how I would survive it. In the end I packed up a few days early and fled, not to the wind-whipped shores of Donegal but to peaceful Galway Bay on the west coast of Ireland. I rode a bicycle and thought about the million starving Irish who had been forced to change their lives nearly a century and a half ago, risking an unknown future in America. And about the descendants of those who stayed behind, unwilling, or unable, to risk any kind of change.

IX

DERRY/LONDONDERRY: STROKE CITY

This ancient walled city with its dark history of violence grew up around a monastery built by St. Columba in the sixth century. The name was originally Doire—"oak grove"—which became Derry. When the city was turned over to craft guilds of London in the seventeenth century, the name was changed from Derry to Londonderry.

The high walls surrounding the heart of the city are an important part of its history. When the Catholic army of King James attacked the Protestant city in 1690, a number of apprentices, young teenage boys, ignored the orders of their elders and slammed shut Bishop's Gate, locking James's soldiers outside the walls, but also trapping the city's 35,000 Protestants inside. The citizens held out against the siege for 105 days. When food supplies were exhausted, the residents ate rats, dogs, cats, candles, and even their leather shoes. Many died from disease and starvation, but still the citizens did not give up. Finally on August 12 the British ships of King William III sailed up the River Foyle and rescued them.

Catholics had always been forced to settle in the boglands outside the wall. Today the River Foyle splits the city into mostly Catholic "Bogside" on one bank and mostly Protestant "Waterside" on the other. The center of the city, within the ancient walls, is holy ground to the Protestants. The modern city has a vast Catholic majority, but Protestants controlled it for years through the process of *gerrymandering*—slicing up Londonderry into voting districts in a way that gave them unfair advantage over the Catholics. In 1966 the 68 percent Catholic population had eight councillors, and the remaining 32 percent, Protestants, had twelve.

Eventually the gerrymander was outlawed, permitting the Catholic majority to take over the Town Council. They promptly resumed using the original name of Derry. Protestants, however, refuse to accept the change and persist in calling it Londonderry. One way to tell "which foot he digs with" is what he calls the city. I sometimes deliberately used the "wrong" name, calling it "Derry" around Protestants and "Londonderry" around Catholics, to see what would happen. Almost invariably I was corrected. But the best alternative I heard was "Stroke City," for the stroke mark (/) used by those who waffle and call it "Derry/Londonderry." It's sometimes written "L'Derry" by people who want to stay neutral.

Whatever it's called, this city has long been a flash point of Northern Ireland. Its reputation is the worst in the country in terms of housing and employment. For a long time it was a textile town with vast linen mills that employed large numbers of women and children. About a quarter of the men are out of work—always have been and probably always will be.

Ever since the Siege of Londonderry, the city has been a symbolic, emotional place for Protestants. Every year some twenty-to-thirty thousand Protestants gather on August 12 to march around the walls, in memory of the Apprentice Boys who slammed the gates and of Good King Billy and his rescuing troops. In 1969 it was the Apprentice Boys' Parade that triggered violent demonstrations, lighting the fuse of the Troubles.

The start of the Troubles was closely tied to the struggle for civil rights in the United States in the 1960s. The nonviolent protests of men like Martin Luther King, Jr., had finally pressured the U.S. government into passing laws that enforced equal protection for blacks as well as whites. "Violence creates bitterness in the survivors and brutality in the destroyers," King said, but just as the civil rights movement in the U.S. was marked by violence, so in Northern Ireland the protests have not always been peaceful. The success of U.S. blacks inspired the Catholics of Northern Ireland to protest their unfair treatment. The first demonstrations were for housing; Catholics had long complained that Protestants got preferential treatment in public housing. Marching has always been a way the people of Northern Ireland have expressed their opinions and beliefs, and in August 1968 about twenty-five hundred people marched in County Tyrone to protest discrimination in housing.

Two months later Catholics marched in Derry and attempted to go through the Diamond at the center of the walled city. That infuriated the Protestants, who had not allowed Catholics to march through their holy ground for years. Violence broke out. People watching television news saw the police attack the marchers, charging into them with their batons. The following winter a group of students from Queen's University, Belfast, organized a civil rights march that was to go from Belfast to L'Derry, a distance of seventy-five miles. The march started peacefully enough, but the marchers were ambushed along the way. When they finally reached L'Derry, rioting broke out in the city. One leader of the marchers was a fiery young student named Bernadette

Devlin. The spring after the march, at the age of twenty-one, she was elected to the British Parliament.

In August, as the violence spread, British troops were called in. But the violence worsened. In February 1971 the Provos shot a British soldier, the first soldier to be killed since the troops arrived. After that the army began to pick up men suspected of violent activities and to intern them indefinitely in prison camps.

"Bloody Sunday": During a civil rights march on January 30, 1972, thirteen unarmed civilians were shot dead in L'Derry. It was not the last of the bloody days. "Bloody Friday": On July 21, 1972, a bomb planted by the Provos in the center of Belfast killed nine people and injured over a hundred more. The killing went on by both the IRA and the Protestant paramilitary groups, always tit for tat, one retaliation for another, despite pleas for an end to violence. Bitterness and brutality were the residue.

Tim McDade

On his way home from school one day in that bloody year of 1972, ten-year-old Tim McDade passed a police station in the Catholic Bogside of Derry. A policeman, crouched behind piles of sandbags, fired a rubber bullet at the schoolboy, later claiming the boy was blocking his view. When Tim regained consciousness, stretched out on a table in the school cafeteria, he was blind.

Tim refused to go away to Belfast to a special school. He taught himself to read Braille in three weeks and learned to get around on his own. He wasn't able to take the eleven-plus exam but chose to go on to secondary school, where motivation is generally much lower than at grammar school. But Tim McDade didn't know about low motivation. Working with tapes and having people read to him, he breezed through his O-levels, passed all his A-levels, earned a university degree, and went into business with his brother.

While he was still in his teens, Tim started working with a group of children at his church who were interested in singing. A girl named Marie helped him. So did his friend Danny, who has been his companion for years, driving him wherever he needs to go, acting as his guide. The children started off singing hymns, but soon they were experimenting with folk music and pop songs. A few years ago Tim married Marie, an attractive woman with a dazzling smile. The children's chorus got better and better.

I sat in on a rehearsal in a tiny hall at the top of the school building behind the church. Thirty-two singers aged nine to twenty-two sat on wooden risers, huddled in their coats in the unheated hall until Marie insisted that they take them off. They were preparing for a Saturday night concert, opening for a popular Irish singer, and Marie was driving them hard to get ready for that performance. Tim in dark glasses played guitar, his friend Danny on electric bass, someone else on keyboard; drums would be added later.

The singers had copied the lyrics from the blackboard into their notebooks, and Marie was working on the three-part harmony. Her method was simple: repetition. Nobody reads music ("I tried," Tim joked), and so Marie sang the line and they sang it after her until the main group had mastered the melody. Then she drilled the high harmony singers, going over and over their part until they had it down. Next she filled in the low harmony.

The song they were practicing was neither Irish nor religious nor popular. It was "Summertime" by American composer George Gershwin. "Summe-er-ti-i-ime," they sang, their harmony close. "Breathe *now*," Marie instructed and then made them begin again. She stopped to point out the two *t's* in "cotton" that must be sung distinctly, "cot-ton." They started over. It sounded fine to me. But Marie made them do it again and again—until she was satisfied and the singers were note-and-letter perfect.

The Town They Loved So Well

Tim McDade, like Father Paul, was a natural organizer of other people's time. He knew exactly where I ought to be going around L'Derry, exactly whom I ought to be meeting. He made the phone calls for me, and then he showed up with his sidekick Danny at the scruffy little hotel where I was staying and drove me around so I could get my bearings. ("There's the police station where I got shot," he said, somehow sensing where we were as we passed a fortresslike structure swathed in barbed wire.) I marked Xs on the map where I was to go. His theory was that with a dry run I would be able to find my way through the maze of crooked streets on my own.

That first afternoon Danny parked the car near the Diamond, and we walked around the old walls, Tim holding on to Danny's elbow. There is graffiti everywhere in Northern Ireland, all sectarian/political, some of it quite well done, some of it merely obscene. The gable-ends of houses in Protestant areas of Belfast display elaborate paintings of King William on a white horse. But most graffitists aren't that talented or subtle. In Protestant areas the messages usually ran to FUCK THE POPE; NOT AN INCH; NO SURRENDER. Catholics scrawl UP THE IRA or UP THE PROVOS. Most of the graffiti in L'Derry was anti-Prod, but here I saw a new one: JAFFA BASTARDS. I understood the second half, but what did "Jaffa" mean?

"It's a kind of orange. You know Jaffa oranges? Refers to the Orangies, naturally," Tim explained.

For the next several days I followed Tim's schedule. But

one afternoon with a little time to explore on my own I strolled around the Diamond and into an art gallery with an exhibit called "The Town We Loved So Well." There were scenes of Derry/Londonderry painted by both Protestant and Catholic artists. Most of the art was pretty and rural—rows of racks with drying peat, the farmer with his cows. A few were charming city scenes. Only a couple were of present-day Stroke City with soldiers and barbed wire. In the background a tape player provided music, the songs of Irish composer Phil Coulter and his most popular composition, "The Town I Loved So Well."

In my memory I will always see
The town that I have loved so well.
Where our school played ball by the gas yard wall,
And we laughed through the smoke and the smell.
Going home in the rain, running up the Dark Lane,
Past the Jail and down behind the Fountain.
Those were happy days, in so many, many ways,
In the town I loved so well.

But when I've returned, how my eyes have burned
To see how a town could be brought to its knees;
By the armoured cars and the bombed-out bars,
And the gas that hangs on to every breeze.
Now the army's installed by that old gas yard wall,
And that damned barbed wire gets higher and higher
With their tanks and their guns, Oh my God what have they done
To the town I loved so well.

The Misfits

"We're the mad ones," said the boy with the carroty hair, grinning. "The mad, mad, mad ones!"

Tim's teacher friend Mike O'Kane thought I'd get more honest responses from his special education section. This is a poor high school in a poor area in Catholic Derry, and the students who were practically blowing the roof off the schoolroom had been identified as "difficult"—they all have emotional problems or other difficulties that make them misfits in a conventional classroom. The school authorities lumped them all together and turned the bunch over to O'Kane. Now O'Kane had turned the bunch over to me and disappeared.

There were about fifteen boys, and two girls who sat far away from the rowdy hoodlums who would not stop shouting and interrupting each other. I asked them to sit down and be quiet so we could talk, but that was not what interested them. Suddenly they turned their attention to one boy who had gone to sit with the girls. "Pansy!" they hooted, flipping their wrists.

Desperate, I pointed at a freckle-faced kid with an earring and asked him his name.

"John."

"John," I said, "you're the sergeant-at-arms. It's your job to maintain order. You decide who may speak and tell the others to keep quiet. Come up and sit by me."

John liked that idea, but as it turned out he was no better at it than I was. With a shrug and a grin he gave up and went back to his buddies. I was, as usual, having trouble with the accents and the fast speech, but I did catch one question as it came flying by: it had to do with spuds, and were they big in America.

Spuds? Were we really talking about potatoes, or were we talking about something else?

"Samantha Fox!" somebody yelled. "Dolly Parton!"

We were not talking about potatoes. While I tried to decide whether to ignore it, censure it, or go along with it, Mike O'Kane appeared. The mayhem stilled instantly at the sound of his quiet voice. I had agreed to pick out four to come with me for a more private conversation. Operating on instinct, I picked John, the sergeant-at-arms, and three others and received a chorus of hoots and jeers from those who weren't invited. The five of us marched to an empty office and closed the door.

"Where's your notebook?" demanded a boy who called himself Doc.

"I don't use one."

"How can you remember what we say?"

"I remember what I need to remember. I write it all down when I get back to my room. And I've got a little notebook with me in case I have to write down a name or something."

"Write down our names," he ordered.

There was himself, Doc, based on his initials, Dick O'Connor. There was Mac, also called Madonna, for the singer; John, who preferred to be called Cookie; and Christy, who seemed satisfied with his own name. I wrote them down. "Now write this down: That we are not all wee gamins with holes in our trousers who have to be sent off to America to be shown the proper way to live. We'll tell you what else to write as we come to it."

"Where are you staying?" Cookie asked. "The Everglades?" That was the most luxurious and touristy of the city's hotels; there were not many to choose from. I described the place I was staying, out in the suburbs, Waterside.

"That's the Blue Tit!" they crowed.

Actually it wasn't, but I knew where they meant, a few blocks up the road with a blue dome that glowed at night.

"That's Jaffa territory," Doc warned. "That place has been blown up a few times. Soldiers used to drink there."

"Write down that Provos means 'Please Remember Our Victory Over Soldiers," Christy said. "And that we are not all Provos."

"But some of us like them," Madonna added. I wrote.

"You know what a redneck is?" Doc asked. "It's from people smacking us on the back of the neck saying 'get out and get a job, get out and get a job.' "

They talked about Protestants without any particular hostility. Madonna said, "I've got a Prod girlfriend."

"What does your family think?"

He shrugged. "Who cares?"

"Write this down," Christy said. "There are two Prod families living near here, and they're all right."

The conversation veered back to the boy they'd labeled a pansy. They began hooting again, imitating his high, effeminate voice, flipping their limp wrists.

"What if you're wrong?" I asked them. "You're making his life miserable. Even if you're right, why torment him?"

They looked at me pityingly. "We're slow learners," Madonna said with an evil grin. "Stupid."

"The hell you are," I said.

Fortunately the other visits Tim had lined up were not so demanding. When I went to his old high school, things were quite different. Red-headed James took seriously his role of rounding up three other boys, of making the proper introductions, and of being sure that our conversation stayed on track.

Some of the topics were familiar: violence on American streets, questions about how Americans celebrate St. Patrick's Day, curiosity about my views of their country, their city, the situation.

"Everybody just goes about their business, never mind the Troubles," Kieran said. "My sister got married right in the midst of bombs going off."

"What are your politics?" I asked.

"Republican," they answered in one voice.

"We dream about how nice it would be to have a united Ireland, but on the other hand the South is so poor! They have a much lower standard of living than we do here. There are no social benefits." This was James, talking soberly.

"What do you think is going to happen?"

"Civil war."

They agreed on that, but they did not agree on whether Catholics from the Republic would come north to help them. "They *hate* us," said Kieran, but James didn't think they did. Not all of them.

"And the IRA?"

"We don't like the shootings," said James, "bombings that kill innocent people. But the IRA keeps a tight control on drugs. Drugs are a big problem in the South, like in America, but not here. The Provos won't let drugs in. The same as they don't put up with minor crime, like mugging old ladies. They operate outside the law."

"Meaning—?"

"Meaning that they kneecap you if they catch you with drugs."

"The RUC should be grateful," Thomas said. "The IRA has taken care of the drug problem in Northern Ireland."

On the Other Side

The problem with having a Catholic as my main contact was that he tended to have primarily Catholic connections. It had happened in Lewistown, and it happened in L'Derry. Tim did his best and sent me to two state schools.

One of them was the only integrated school in L'Derry, although it hadn't started out that way. Mr. Carlton, the principal, an affable man with an interest in complicated clocks that ticked loudly in his office, explained that the population shift of Protestants away from the area in this part of Londonderry was followed by an influx of Catholics. Children were walking past this large, underused secondary school on their way to crowded Catholic schools. The parents decided to let them attend. The bishop made no objection.

"Why didn't he object?"

"Practical reasons. It was that or build a new school."

Mr. Carlton claimed there was no friction in his school, and I wanted to believe that. He enjoyed telling the story of sending children off on a holiday scheme that required equal numbers of Prods and RCs. There was room for one more Protestant and he had one Catholic boy who badly wanted to go—so they both pretended the boy was Methodist, and off he went.

It was exam time here too, and the only students who were free were a couple of Catholic girls more interested in talking about clothes and discos than in shocking me. One, who planned to go to art school, had wildly disheveled hair and wore an old tuxedo jacket. Her friend had smooth blond hair cut very short on one side, long on the other. She dressed stylishly in tight yellow leggings, a baggy yellow and white shirt, and a huge black coat. If they passed their O-levels—they wouldn't find out their grades until mid-August—then they thought they might go across the street to the grammar school to work toward A-levels.

The school across the street was Foyle & Londonderry, "very upmarket," according to Tim, catering to the cream of L'Derry's crop—mostly Protestant. Only about 20 of the 350 students in the junior school are Catholic. Somebody had spray-painted out the "London" part of the name on the sign at the edge of the lawn that sweeps down to the road. Gazing out over the lawn is the statue of a Notable Person, turning green. The four Third Formers (eighth-graders) who had been collared by the principal didn't know who the Person was.

I tried that question as an opener, and it didn't work. These fourteen-year-olds clearly did not want to be here. They perched anxiously on folding chairs in a large empty room, all dressed in the school uniform, maroon blazers with the school crest on the pocket: sword, owl, castle, and book.

Melissa, swinging her feet, whispered that her father is a policeman. An Indian boy, whose name I could not catch, mumbled that he lives on a farm. He was born in Northern Ireland after his parents moved here in the 1960s. (There is a large Indian population in Northern Ireland, people who emigrated at a time when the area was considered a land of opportunity.) Larry, in thick round glasses, stared at his shoes and said nothing. The third boy, Rod, stared at me and said nothing. For fifteen minutes I struggled to get them to say something, *anything*, when abruptly all four announced that their buses were leaving. They walked carefully to the door like people who really wanted to run.

The principal hurried by a few minutes later and found me studying the trophies displayed in glass cases in the lobby. "How did it go?" he asked me.

"It didn't."

Youth Center: Bogside

There is a modern, well-equipped youth center in a dismal part of town near the police barracks where Tim McDade was shot. The government has built such centers all over Northern Ireland, trying to find a place to go for the thousands of unemployed young people whose lives are built on the Bru. Tim sent me to a friend who, for the umpteenth time since my arrival in Northern Ireland, shut me up in a room with a group of people only minimally interested in meeting "an American lady who's writing a book," but so bored that any kind of distraction, even a lady writer, was better than nothing.

People constantly barged into the room, looking for somebody or simply wanting to see what was going on. Finally one of the boys blocked the door with his chair; people outside banged and yelled, trying to force it open. He managed to keep it shut, but I expected it to burst off its hinges any second. The door held, but the racket was deafening.

This was another tough bunch. They wanted to know how I got there, to Derry, to the Youth Center, and when I told them I had a hired car they began badgering me to take them to Donegal, less than an hour's drive west of here. They were about nineteen or twenty years old, and because of their age or for some other reason—it didn't seem to be lack of cash—it was easier for me to rent a car than it was for them.

"Please, Miss!" they insisted loudly. "We'll stay in a hostel or camp out, and you can stay wherever you like. We'll buy the gas, we'll show you around, we'll pay part of the car rental. Just take us to Donegal! Take us, take us, miss!" I was sorry I had mentioned the car.

There was the usual jockeying for attention, but finally they settled down a little and talked about being on the Bru, collecting £25 (about $37) a week from age sixteen on, or getting a little more than that to take YTP classes. A few were in YTP, one studying welding and fabricating, another, a heavyset fellow with an air of confidence, learning salesmanship. He seemed to believe he actually would get a job as a salesman, and he was unruffled when the others laughed at him, jeering cynically. Everybody knows that nobody gets a job from YTP training.

Every other word, it seemed was "fuck": "fuckin' this" and "fuckin' that," and the more at ease they seemed to feel around me, the more foul their language became. They began to argue at the top of their voices about whether Lewistown, which I had just come from, was RC or Prod, everyone shouting the "F" word. I had had enough, and I shouted over their roar, "It's 60 percent fuckin' Catholic and 40 percent fuckin' Prod!"

Stunned, they shut up instantly. I was a little embarrassed. The conversation continued in a more docile manner.

"I'd just like to know, miss, are you Catholic or Protestant?" one asked finally, in a formal way.

"Take a guess."

They all guessed Catholic.

"Why do you think I'm Catholic?"

"Because you're so. . . ." They didn't finish the sentence, as it dawned on them that I was Protestant. They seemed uneasy, even apologetic, for having been so open with somebody from the other side.

As I was leaving one of them followed me. "Let me drive your car, miss," he said.

"I can't." I had heard too much about kids "borrowing" cars for joyrides.

"Just around the block. Just around the car park," he pleaded.

"I'm sorry, but my insurance won't allow it." Probably sounded as lame to him as it did to me, but there was no way I was going to turn my car over to this guy. He walked away without a word.

Dancing: Waterside

A children's disco? What on earth is a children's disco?

Whatever it was, it was happening in the basement of my hotel. Teenagers from a nearby Protestant housing estate crowded into the downstairs nightclub, where a slowly revolving mirrored ball spattered drops of colored light on the floor and walls. Blinking red and white Christmas lights outlined the pillars. Heaps of empty soft drink cans cluttered the tables. Slow music blasted. A half-dozen couples were "dancing," locked in each other's arms, shifting their weight from foot to foot as though their shoes were nailed to the floor. When the music swung up-tempo, the couples fled and hordes of girls in gaudy clothes surged out and began to dance.

This disco was for the "under sixteens," according to the woman selling tickets at the door—meaning they were probably twelve. "Under eighteen" means maybe fourteen, and so on. "They're always trying to sneak in to the next highest age level," she said.

The next night the mood changed. A group called "Memphis," dressed in American western-style shirts and boots, played American-style country and western music. At ten o'clock I went downstairs to see what was going on. Not much at that hour, but slowly the place filled up and the music began. There were some local singing acts: a huge fat man named Big Daddy, and a wizened old fellow in an elaborately embroidered cowboy shirt who danced a little jig.

An elderly couple celebrating their wedding anniversary arrived with their married children and took over several upholstered booths. The women in the group, all dressed up in longish dresses and spike heels, rushed giggling out onto the dance floor and executed a free-form kind of partnerless dance that bore no resemblance to country and western. Gradually their husbands drifted out to dance with them. *Shuffle shuffle,* they went, not in time with the music, around and around the floor.

A young man with a shorter-than-usual haircut and highly polished laced-up shoes deftly danced the twist from the 1950s. Clearly he was a soldier, maybe one of those who stood in the middle of the Limavady Road a couple of blocks from this hotel, watching a dangerous intersection through the sights of his rifle.

On my way out I spoke to one of the local singers, a man named Ian Lloyd. "The only place I want to go in the whole U.S.A. is Nashville," he said fervently.

Sex and Socks

Only one more school to visit and I could get out of L'Derry. I had been in far more schools in Northern Ireland than I had ever intended, and I did not want to sit in front of one more bunch of kids who would either stare at the floor or punch each other and swear or tell me things I had heard several times before. In this state of mind I almost skipped going to the Catholic grammar school. But Tim McDade heard the tone of my voice and said, "Go to this one. It's different."

He was right: it *was* different. A girls' school with some thirteen hundred students, it sported manicured lawns, polished hallways, everything in top condition. A teacher named Joe Reilly with a gray beard and sandals led me to the teachers' lounge for a cup of tea before taking me to meet the girls, all from English classes.

"How many?"

"About forty," he said. "Will that be enough?"

"Four would be better," I said. Miss Rogers, one of Joe's colleagues, went to see if she could pare down the number.

"These students are all studying for A-levels," Joe said. "English is a popular subject, because it's easier to pass than, say, physics. And many girls want to stay in school as long as possible, even if they're not really academically inclined, because of the job situation."

Miss Rogers came back. "I could only get it down to thirteen," she said. "The others agreed to leave, but these thirteen insist that they want to meet with you."

So thirteen it was, scattered around a classroom. My heart was not in this. Outside the sun was beaming, and I was yearning to be away. Nevertheless I wobbled through the usual preliminaries, telling them a little about who I was and what my writing was about, and asking them about themselves.

"Will you stay in Derry when you finish school?"

The replies were about evenly divided. Half of them wanted to go from university to jobs in Dublin, London, Canada, Australia; one of them was thinking about the U.S. The others saw themselves coming back to live in Derry, even though job opportunities are virtually nil.

"Is Derry a good place to bring up children?"

That prompted a lively debate. "It's very narrow here," one girl said. "Not just sectarian, but people are opposed to any kind of change. They hate new ideas."

"It's a very tight community," someone else pointed out. "Everybody knows everybody. The grannies can track each other's families back for generations, who's related to who."

"There's no privacy! Everybody knows everybody else's business!"

"But there's not much crime here. It's safe to walk on the streets. Not like New York! Not like London!"

We talked about women's rights; rather, *they* talked and I listened. Northern Ireland is not a place where women's rights are an issue, and I had in fact read that both men and women are threatened by professional women who have successful careers, believing there is something "unnatural" about such a woman. But these girls were not at all reticent. They began by griping about the preferential treatment demanded by their brothers and fathers; the girls are expected to do all the chores. Gradually, as we were talking, they had all moved to seats closer to each other and to me, and they warmed to the subject. They thought women were treated better by men in the Republic than they were in Northern Ireland.

"A woman can go into a pub in the South and the men will all buy her drinks. They won't do that here. They don't think a woman has any business being in a pub," said Maureen, a fiery girl with thick dark hair that she raked with her hands as she talked. "She should be at home fixing his tea."

"Women's rights doesn't mean having men buy you drinks in bars," retorted Paula, a tall girl with a definite manner. "It means being treated with respect as a person."

"What do you see as the primary issue?"

"Equal pay for equal work."

I told them that many married working women in the U.S. complain that they still have to do most of the housework and take primary responsibility for child care.

"Not in the family I stayed with," said Kate, who had been to America as part of the Channels of Peace program. "My host family shared all the chores equally."

That got us onto Channels of Peace. Several of the girls had been involved when they were fifteen, two years ago, and they were not optimistic about the long-range results. "At first we all got along fine, but as we got into those breakthrough sessions, the Prods got angry. They withdrew completely. They wouldn't even sit with us on the plane coming home."

"Have you kept in contact since then?"

"For a while we tried to have monthly meetings, but the Prods refused to come Bogside and we got tired of going Waterside every month, and after a while we just quit trying and it all fell apart."

"Typical Prod," said Maureen. "I dated a Prod boy for five months. He came to my house, and he was always welcomed. But I was never invited to his house. He kept me a secret from his family."

Comments flew from all sides:

"Most of the Prods live Waterside, but there are some

Catholic areas over there as well. The police like to do ID checks on Sunday morning before mass. They stop everyone on their way to church and make them all late. They do it on purpose, of course, to harass us."

"Prod boys are awful. When they see a group of Catholic girls they yell at us, 'You're all virgins, you haven't been fucked yet, you need a good fuck!' and give us the finger. But there are probably more Prod virgins than there are Catholic virgins."

"A lot of teenage girls get pregnant. Some in the estates have two or three babies before they're married."

"More Catholics than Protestants get pregnant before they're married. That's because it's a sin to use birth control."

"But premarital sex is a sin, too," said sensible Paula. "So if you're committing that one you'd better use birth control as well and sin *responsibly*."

"Prod girls are terrible. They have to have everything perfect. Their mummies choose their clothes and comb their hair for them. Every hair has to be in place. And they're very prudish."

"They say you can tell a Catholic girl by her socks," Maureen said.

"Her socks?"

"They say we're sloppy. That our socks are always falling down. A Protestant girl's socks never look like that."

"Are you suggesting," I joked, "that you can tell a virgin by her *socks*?"

We were still giggling over the possibilities of that when the door opened and Joe came in to see what was going on with his English class. "Oh oh," I said. "We'd better pull up our socks, girls."

I had been scheduled to stay only a short time, but we were having a great time and nearly two hours had flown by. For once I was in no hurry to leave.

X

COUNTY ARMAGH: THE PIP IN THE MIDDLE

Renaissance House

Ballyfergus—not its real name—is an ordinary town in an extreme situation. "The most divided town in Northern Ireland," said Charlie Cooper—not his real name either. "The dividing line is at the public toilets." He drove past the toilets on an island in the middle of the main street. "Everything north of here is Protestant, and everything south is Catholic. People from one side rarely cross to the other."

Charlie is the director of Renaissance House, a community center that provides programs for people of all ages and backgrounds. When I met him in Belfast he had invited me to come down and see what it was like. "The town is like two halves of an apple," he told me then, "and we're the pip in the middle."

It was easy to tell which was which. The Prod side had signs and banners strung up everywhere: BALLYFERGUS

STILL SAYS NO. Renaissance House, a rabbit warren of a place, its seedy, rundown rooms and halls painted brave, bright colors, was located one block into Protestant turf. That created problems. Catholics didn't want to go there, and Prods didn't want them to come there. Charlie hired both Protestant and Catholic workers, but the Prods criticized him for hiring too many RCs and threatened to "put him out of business" if the balance swung the "wrong way"—too many Catholics. Charlie tries to convince people that the center is meant for everybody.

"It's hard to get the Protestants to participate in peace and reconciliation projects like this one," Charlie said. "They don't have a history of joining self-help groups and bootstrap operations."

Charlie himself walks a fine line; he has been personally threatened several times and the Renaissance vans have been continually vandalized, windows bashed in.

"Who does it?"

He shrugged. "Could be either side."

I got roped into helping with the decorations for the disco at Town Hall being put on for a group of twenty girls visiting from the Republic. One of the Renaissance staff, Brian Conlon, climbed a ladder, and I dug through cartons of tattered Christmas decorations, handing bits of tinsel up to him to fasten to crossbeams. I was not sure why we were doing this; the effect was forlorn rather than festive.

Soon the girls began to troop in, decked out in various kinds of dress-up. One thirteen-year-old girl modeled a broad-brimmed hat, a flowered dress, very high heels, and a slash of bright red lipstick; she destroyed her sophisticated image by chomping on a wad of gum. Most of the others were into punk—ultrashort skirts, colored hairspray, heavy metal jewelry.

Brian finished hooking up an impressive sound system, disappeared into a toilet, and emerged in black tights and a black shirt, his face clown white. Charlie sauntered in wearing kilts, tartan sash, nonmatching tartan scarf, and sagging socks and offered to paint the face of anyone who came through the door. At first the decorated faces were fairly restrained, but as the evening wore on, the girls took over the painting and the style got wilder. They spied my unadorned face, pounced on me, and painted everything blue; I had blue paint in my nose and ears and mouth. I kept my eyes squinted shut.

Charlie tried to organize some games with a parachute that produced shrieking and giggling; musical chairs turned out to be fairly rowdy as well. But mostly the girls wanted to dance, and for a couple of hours they did, stopping occasionally to drag on cigarettes—nearly all of them smoked—and to watch themselves on video. Charlie had set up a TV set and walked around capturing their silliness with a video camera. By 10:30 the floor was littered with empty crisp bags and soda cans, and a half-dozen girls were stretched out flat on rows of chairs at the side of the dance floor, sound asleep.

Feeding the Crowd

Charlie's right-hand woman, Catherine Wellborn, was in charge of taking me around, but like the rest of the staff of Renaissance, she had too much to do and too little time to do it.

"It's not a job," she told me as we stopped by the bakery to pick up baps and farls—white rolls and soda bread. "It's a way of life. Charlie works seven days a week, and most of the time I do too. It's a good thing his wife works there, or they'd never see each other."

We raced toward Town Hall, carrying baps, farls, and cartons of milk to prepare lunch for the elderly. "Would you have some time to help out?" Catherine asked. "All the volunteers are out today, and Geraldine can't handle it all alone."

They didn't expect a big crowd that day, because there were a number of weddings in town ("Poor fools," snorted Catherine, single and cynical about marriage) to which many of the old people were invited. The biggest turnout is always Tuesday—bingo day.

While Geraldine prepared the soup from a mix, I set the table for thirty pensioners and the twenty visiting teenage girls who might or might not show up. Some of them were supposed to help as part of a "service project." I served the soup and dished up ice cream and peaches, and when there was a moment I sat down at a table with some of the old people to eat my own lunch. One of the women collected the fee from each one at her table; the rest helped to clear, scooting the empty dishes across the smooth surface to another woman who stacked them. The butter whizzed by, followed by the sugar. They watched me watching them and laughed. "Don't put *this* in your book!" One thing I *do* want to put in my book, though, is that these people in their sixties and seventies eating lunch and talking and joking together were both Catholic and Protestant. Somehow their sectarian differences were no longer important.

The kitchen was backbreakingly inefficient. There was no place to put leftovers, because the refrigerator was tiny, barely apartment size. The dishwasher was broken and the sink apparently built for midgets. After an hour of bending over it, up to my elbows in hot soapy water, I could barely straighten up. The visiting girls had swooped in, scarfed down their lunches, and disappeared again.

Geraldine, the soupmaker, is a young field-worker who visits the elderly in their homes and works in the kitchen fixing lunch four or five days a week. She and her husband, who also works for Renaissance, have a little daughter who stays with her grandmother while Geraldine works. Geraldine tries to spend weekends with the child. But this was Renaissance—"A way of life, not a job"—and it was hard to find a clear weekend. Her husband used to complain about the time she was devoting to community work until he got involved in it too.

Besides this job, Geraldine is co-leader of a Protestant youth club. "A few weeks ago a stranger was spotted in the housing estate near the club," she told me. "Someone came in and said, 'There's a Catholic in the area!' and the kids grabbed whatever they could get their hands on to go out and attack him. Mostly fourteen- and fifteen-year-old boys. They're the worst, the angriest. It was just desperate! Beth Shipley and I managed to lock the doors and keep them all inside. And it turned out it wasn't a Catholic after all—just somebody they didn't know."

There's blind hatred between the two groups, she said. Once some of the boys threatened to petrol bomb Catherine Wellborn's car. They thought she was Catholic. Scared her half to death.

"They don't know each other, the RC and Prod kids. They've never actually met," Geraldine said. "And the parents feed the hatred. We try to take the kids on trips so they'll get to know each other and politics can be forgotten for a while and maybe won't even be so important when they're home again, but the parents interfere. We end up cancelling the trips because one side or the other won't let the kids go. I blame the politicians. They have a stake in keeping things boiling. All they care about is power."

I was mopping the kitchen floor when Catherine came to collect me. "We're taking the girls from the South out to the shopping center in the van," she said. "You might as well ride along."

The van was filled with smoke and raucous screeches. I

sat in the back with eight girls who were passing a "wee butt" around. Every now and then one or another would lean across me and wallop somebody. Later Catherine asked if I wanted to go along the next day on the trip to the Antrim Coast. I said "No thanks."

But whoever was supposed to pack the lunches for the trip to the Antrim Coast had failed to show up, and it looked as though the job would fall to Catherine—as usual. I volunteered, although I didn't relish the idea of spending more time in the kitchen. I was staying with George and Beth Shipley and their chubby baby, Billy. George and Beth were hoping for a night out, and I had already told them I'd babysit. I could make sandwiches while Billy slept.

Catherine dropped off eight loaves of bread, a dozen eggs, sacks of lettuce and tomatoes, packages of luncheon meat. "Make as many meat as you can, the rest egg and onion or salad." She left before I could ask all the questions I thought of later: What is an egg and onion sandwich? If it's like egg salad, is it held together with salad cream (the Ulster word for mayonnaise)? What's a "salad" sandwich? If it's lettuce and tomato, is it thick or thin? Seasoned? How much? I had visions of the young Irish ladies chucking weird American-style sandwiches out the van windows as—*biff!bam!socko!*—they continued to slug it out with each other. It was midnight when I finished and collapsed into bed. I had managed to make the ingredients come out even, and at that point I didn't care if the girls liked them or not.

Unwinding

Charlie and Laura Cooper live a few blocks from Renaissance, across the street from the Shipleys in an old house. Their cozy living room with the coal-burning fireplace in the middle and some of Laura's paintings on the walls is a gathering place for people from Renaissance House looking for a place to unwind.

Brian Conlon and his girlfriend Nancy stopped by. Brian was in a group with Charlie that visited the U.S. the previous spring, and they talked about how their TV image of America was shattered by soup kitchens and Skid Row down-and-outers in New York. Now Brian was seething with frustration. He's a big, bearish, dark-haired man with a tiny loop earring, and he was furious about the things he couldn't get done for Renaissance House. His job description is "peace worker," but he has no chance to do peace work, he said, because he's Catholic. When he calls a Prod on the phone to ask for something, he usually says he's Charlie Cooper, because Charlie is known to be a Protestant. And when Charlie talks to an RC, he pretends he's Brian. "We do whatever we have to do to get the job done."

Nancy didn't say much about their relationship, but Brian did. They met in a pub—he thought she was Catholic, but she knew right off he wasn't Protestant—and have been going out together for seven weeks. "This is the way it ought to be between Prods and RCs," he said, patting her hand. But it isn't that simple: her family objects, although his does not, and they have to be very careful where they go together. If it comes to marriage, they would have trouble finding a neutral place to live.

"What do you want for your country?" I asked him.

"A united Ireland seems like a nice idea, but it would be an economic disaster," he said. "Meanwhile, everything seems to be getting worse here."

Charlie seconded that. "The Anglo-Irish agreement has polarized people. Now the police are another enemy. The RUC community-relations workers here can't do anything now. They sit on top of a bomb."

Ballyfergus has had its share of tragedy during the Troubles; the latest hit squarely at home when one of the staff members of Renaissance House was killed by a plastic bullet. A few weeks earlier, twenty-year-old Larry had gone to an Apprentice Boys' parade in a nearby town, celebrating the day in 1690 the boys had slammed shut the gates of Londonderry. He was unaware that the RUC had canceled the Protestant parade. Violence broke out; the police fired into the crowd; Larry was struck, lay in a coma for two weeks, and died.

His parents made public pleas for no retaliations, no violence. Larry was the first Protestant to be killed by a plastic bullet, and his parents called for a ban on their use. Everybody seemed to have something to say about the tragedy. Ian Paisley attended the funeral. Politicians demanded inquiries. The RUC got the blame—for banning the parade (some called it a "Dublin-inspired ban," meaning that the Republic of Ireland was somehow responsible) and for firing the bullet. And everybody on the Protestant side of town blamed the Anglo-Irish agreement, demanding that it be scrapped "before the situation gets completely out of hand."

Conversation switched to a postmortem on the trip with the girls from the South, who apparently disappointed—and angered—everybody. Catherine had spent an entire day chauffeuring them from place to place: to a shopping center, to a roller skating rink, to another community center. Charlie had spent most of his day replacing a broken window in the back of the Renaissance bus, but the girls had broken it again on the way back from skating. They had to round up another bus at the last minute to go to Antrim.

"All day long they went on and on about getting to the beach, and when we got there, they refused to move from the bus," Charlie said. "I gave up. I lay down on the beach and went to sleep. All they thought about was getting back in time to have another disco."

These kids were undisciplined and immature, Charlie said. They wanted to run around, spend money, and meet boys. They did not want to sit down and discuss the differences between the North and the South. Entertaining themselves may have been the reason why the girls from the Republic had made the long trip up here, but that wasn't why Charlie and his staff were knocking themselves out.

Since all the girls were Catholics, they had to stay with Catholic families in Ballyfergus; they were not meeting Protestants, and there was no learning going on. They had to be watched constantly to keep them out of Prod areas—not easy to do, since Renaissance is one block into Protestant territory. They didn't understand that Northern Ireland is a dangerous place. "Some of those kids had never been away from home before," Charlie's wife Laura said mildly. "They're not interested in talking about why life in the North is different from life where they come from."

There was no word on what they thought of my sandwiches.

As usual, Charlie had to leave and run over to Renaissance, which gave Laura a chance to tell me about their marriage. She met Charlie at a dance in Cookstown where she lived, about halfway between Ballyfergus and Lewistown. "Ten years ago Cookstown was famous for its dances. And there was Charlie. My parents didn't quite approve of him—they considered it a 'mixed marriage,' because our family is CofI and Charlie's is Presbyterian. And he didn't seem to know what he wanted to do. I kept telling my father, 'Whatever it is he does, he'll be good at it.' He had a business for a while, but he was always involved with kids. There was always a queue of young teenage boys at the door: 'Charlie, can we wash your car?' They were like *slaves*. Then those boys would grow up and get interested in girls and drift away, and they'd be replaced by other boys. It's still like that, except now it's full time, all the time."

Across the street my host, George Shipley, had just come home from the club where he moonlights as a bartender. He is glad to have that second job—glad to have the *first* one, as a matter of fact—but he said he'd be just as well off financially if he were on the Bru and collected allowances for housing, clothes, medical care. He and Charlie Cooper are friends; George told me he sometimes hears talk from men at the club that if Charlie allows too many of the "other kind" around Renaissance House, the men will destroy it in a moment. Charlie knows that.

George used to travel when he was young and single, and he reminisced about being kicked out of Switzerland for his loud all-night partying. "They told me not to come back until I was married with a family," he said. George had already had several beers, and he popped another one. "Have you ever noticed," he asked me, "that all the rubbish countries are Catholic controlled?"

Rubbish countries?

"Like Italy and Spain. Filthy messes. What I can't understand," he said, "is how the Vatican with all its wealth can allow the countries they control, Peru and Bolivia, for instance, to be so rubbishy, with thieves on every corner. It proves that Catholics are messy."

I knew better than to get into debates like this one, but I did anyway. "Poland and Czechoslovakia are predominantly Catholic," I suggested, "and they're not trashy."

"That," George said, "is because the Communists are in charge, and they're more powerful than the Pope. Communists don't allow thievery and garbage on the streets. The Pope does."

Sunday Morning, Sunday Afternoon

Sunday morning. The streets were empty. The Shipleys showed no inclination to go to church, and I had not yet made up my mind whether I was going to be a Catholic or a Protestant that day. Then I heard band music, and when I went outside to investigate I found the Salvation Army Band marching down the street, tooting a hymn. That decided it: I followed them to their mission a few blocks away.

Of the roughly 150 people present, 100 were in the black, Salvation Army uniform, the women in the black bonnets with a big bow under the chin. Besides the brass band there was a grand piano and a small organ, a children's choir and a large adult choir. There was plenty of music before the sermon. The message was peace, focused on South Africa. The next day would be the tenth anniversary of the Soweto Uprising, and the TV and newspapers of Northern Ireland had been full of news of trouble in that part of the world—riots and killings, a new state of emergency, proposed sanctions. I was constantly reminded of my visit to South Africa nine months earlier. At that time I had watched television in Johannesburg and Cape Town and listened to reports of violence in Northern Ireland.

Sunday afternoon. I took a walk around town, down the deserted main street where all the shops were closed, and ran into Catherine. We went out for lunch and then strolled over to a park by a lake. The sun was shining—maybe at last it was summer!—and the residents of Ballyfergus had stripped off as many clothes as they decently could and were sprawled everywhere, soaking up the ultraviolet rays and turning bright pink. People in Northern Ireland, particularly those with Celtic genes, have little melanin in their skin that allows it to tan; they burn fast, and they're more prone to develop skin cancer than practically anyone else in the world.

In this rainy, gray climate there would seem not to be much risk of overexposure. On a rare day like this, no one was being cautious.

Catherine and I sat by a stream and watched children get wet despite their parents' warnings. She told me about her dreams for Renaissance House. Last year they had sponsored a "duck race" with numbered plastic ducks floating down this stream into the lake. This year they bought plastic dolphins, but ticket sales weren't going well for the "race." Charlie called a staff meeting exhorting his people to get out and sell tickets. Then he called a staff meeting to find ways to relieve workers like Catherine and Geraldine and Brian of some of their heavy duties, but somehow they all left the meeting with even more responsibilities than they had when they came. Next week they were planning a dinner at Town Hall as another fund-raiser. Catherine would probably end up doing most of the cooking.

"Want to stay around another few days, Caroline?" she asked. "You're good in the kitchen."

I had to say no. It was time to get back to Belfast. The next morning the train was already pulling into the station when Catherine came puffing along the platform, hugged me, and thrust a little package into my hand. I opened it on the train: a white china thimble decorated with green shamrocks, symbol of Ireland. "Good luck," the card said.

I needed Irish luck. But they need it a lot more.

XI

BELFAST: OTHER TRIBES

The Royal Ulster Constabulary

"There are three tribes in Northern Ireland," someone told me, "Catholics, Protestants, and police." It sounded glib at the time, but the more I heard, the more I believed it was true.

There was a time when the Royal Ulster Constabulary—the police—seemed to be on the side of the Protestants against the Catholics. Most RUC people are Protestant; few Catholics join the police force. But since the signing of the Anglo-Irish agreement, Protestants have come to believe that the RUC is no longer on their side. I called the RUC's main number and asked to come and visit. After my experience at Harland and Wolff, I was ready for anything.

I expected RUC headquarters to be like other stations around Belfast and elsewhere in the country, secured behind formidable walls festooned with barbed wire. But this place was located in a pretty suburb surrounded by grass and purple rhododendrons, more like a college campus. The taxi left me at the guardhouse where several men gazed at TV monitors. A phone call was made, and one of the men walked with me up the hill to the main building. From there a receptionist escorted me through labyrinthine corridors to the office of Superintendent Malcolm Bell (not his real name). Bell is a tall, good-looking, friendly man who ordered tea, lit a cigarette, and invited me to ask questions.

Just then a woman in the dark green uniform of the RUC rushed in, hastily fastening on her insignia, calling Bell "sir," and apologizing for being late. Bell made the introductions —Florence something—and I suddenly could not remember if his rank was inspector or superintendent and which was higher. If I called him "Inspector Bell," was I giving him a promotion or a demotion? He came to the rescue: "Call me Malcolm."

Between the two of them they were able to supply any facts and figures I could ask for. In addition, Bell handed me a packet of materials filled with statistics for the previous year: That there are 8,237 members of the force, 644 of them women. That in 1985 twenty-three officers, three of them young women constables, were murdered by terrorists. That of the 1,897 Loyalist and 223 Republican parades and demonstrations policed by the RUC in 1985, only two were banned and fifteen rerouted. That in the same year the Provisional IRA attacked thirteen RUC stations with bombs and mortars, killing eleven members and destroying or severely damaging several buildings. That the number of vehicles stolen in 1985 increased over the year before to a total of 6,998, 77 percent of them in West Belfast by juvenile "joyriders." Brightly colored bar graphs illustrated five years of terrorist activity: murders, attempted murders, bombings. The bars for the "Republicans" were longer than those for the "Loyalists."

"Why would anybody want to join the police force with

statistics like these, and hated by both sides?" Obviously it's a dangerous occupation; I remembered Donny in the restaurant a few weeks earlier, speaking softly about the risks of his work. And the superintendent had just told me about the seven years he served in an area of West Belfast known to be one of the hottest of the flash points.

"Most new recruits give idealistic reasons, like serving the community and helping people. But the real answer is here." Bell handed me a sheet outlining the wage structure. Police work is one of the best paid and most financially secure jobs in Northern Ireland, with wages much higher for a new constable joining the force than most college graduates could hope to earn—provided they could find a job.

For this reason, the RUC is at full strength with far more applicants than can be accepted. Virtually all of them are Protestant; Catholics would be harassed by their communities for siding with the "enemy." Young men and women can apply at eighteen. They don't need any academic qualifications, but they must pass a series of tests and interviews. Training lasts fourteen weeks, and for the next two years they alternate practical experience with course work. They are trained immediately in the use of firearms—pistol, revolver, rifle, Sterling submachine gun—and all of them are issued small arms, like a pistol, to carry even off-duty in case of trouble. They also carry batons (pronounced BAT'ns), short wooden clubs.

Right now the RUC is much criticized for the use of plastic bullets, the kind that killed the young man in Ballyfergus. "But it's the only thing we have for riot control," Bell said. "When kids start throwing rocks and petrol bombs, the police are sometimes caught in the cross fire between Catholics and Protestants trying to get at each other. The plastic bullet is meant to hurt. It shouldn't kill you, but you'll know you've been hit and you won't come back for more."

"But they *do* kill. And they *do* blind."

"True. But they're still better than live ammunition. Batons are only good in one-on-one situations. They don't work for mob violence. If they take away the plastic bullets, then they have to give us something else."

"Like what?"

"That's the problem. There is nothing else."

I ventured a question about drug control. Did he want to give any credit to the Provisional IRA for keeping drugs out of the North? Of course I knew the answer was no. What else could he say? "It's because of our big drug squads," he said. "The numbers were increased, not because drug abuse showed signs of getting out of hand, but because we're determined that this must never be allowed to happen. So far we've managed to avoid the problems you have in America and the U.K."

One problem they have indeed managed to keep under control is street crime, particularly crimes of violence against women. (Although some give the IRA credit for that, too.) Rape, for example, is far less common in Northern Ireland than it is in the U.S. I was never afraid to walk alone at night in Belfast; I would not dream of doing that in my own city.

But one problem the RUC has not avoided is the problem of being mistrusted and hated by almost everybody.

The Peace People

I already knew the first part of the story: in August 1976, three children were killed by a runaway car. Behind the wheel of the car was an IRA man, shot dead by British soldiers. One of the witnesses to the accident was a woman named Betty Williams, who that night saw the children's aunt, Mairead Corrigan, interviewed on television. Betty got in touch with Mairead, and both contacted others. More women joined them. Petitions were circulated. The day after the funeral some ten thousand women demonstrated, some of them Protestants from the Shankill and from East Belfast.

In that way the peace movement was born, led by Mairead and Betty and a third person, journalist Ciaran McKeown. Mairead was a secretary for Guinness Brewery, single, living at home with her parents, active in church work. Betty was the wife of a seaman who was away most of the time, the mother of two children. And Ciaran, who had a pregnant wife and four children, was the Belfast correspondent of a British newspaper. All three were in their thirties. Each brought a different personality and a different talent to the peace movement—Mairead the spiritual one, Betty the practical one, Ciaran the educated intellectual.

There were problems with the peace movement in its early days. It began spontaneously, without much organization, and so much—too much—was expected of it. Each of those involved had a personal notion of what "peace" meant—and the notions were all different. Most people wanted the kind of peace that required no personal or national sacrifices. Still, it was a new way of thinking in Ulster. People were often critical of the movement, but the efforts of Betty and Mairead earned them the Nobel Peace Prize in 1976. (Ciaran, who was always in the background of the organization, did not share in the prize.)

The peace movement has had no apparent effect on terrorism, but it did—and does—have an effect on the people involved in it. Ten years later the Community of the Peace People is still alive, but it has changed. Some of the original people are no longer involved, and most of the attention the group now gets from the outside world is focused on the gossip: Betty Williams divorced her seaman husband, remarried, and went to Florida to start a new life. Mairead's sister, the mother of the children killed ten years ago, had two more children, sank into a depression, and committed suicide. Mairead went to help her brother-in-law care for his children, later married him, and had two babies of her own. Ciaran, once a respected journalist, works for a printer; he became so controversial during the early days of the peace movement that no newspaper would hire him—and he now has seven children to support. Mairead Corrigan Maguire nominated rock musician Bob Geldof, who made headlines with his organization of Band-Aid and Sport-Aid to combat world hunger, for the 1986 Nobel Peace Prize.

One of the first people to go to work for the Peace People in 1976 was Carleen, who started off as a part-time typist. Her children were young then, and her husband wanted her to stay at home. They agreed that she would work part-time for six weeks, then six more weeks. Now she's the head administrator and sometimes wishes she had a nine-to-five job with no problems. Her husband is not involved with the Peace People. "He's an ardent Republican," Carleen said, "but completely nonviolent."

The Peace People are headquartered in a large brick house named "Fredheim House," meaning *peace* in Norwegian. The money to purchase the house came from Norway, but it's a struggle to maintain it. "When it rains and blows I run outside to see how many slates have been ripped off the roof," Carleen said.

It wasn't like this in 1976 when money began to pour in from all over the world. Some money still comes in from a college in the U.S., but most outside sources have dried up. Eventually people began to ask questions: What happens to all the money that's been donated? It's the same questions people were asking about Bob Geldof and the money his projects raised. Many assume that the founders got rich, took their money, and ran. The criticism upsets Carleen. I passed along to her one of my favorite mottos: "No good deed goes unpunished." She laughed and wrote it down.

Despite financial problems, the Peace People are alive and well and active. They own a minibus and take wives and families to visit men held as political prisoners far from Belfast. At first the IRA was against it, breaking bus windows and slashing tires and scaring the Catholics into not riding the bus. For a while only Protestants used the service, but little by little the IRA eased off, and Catholic women began to go along. Now the wives have established friendships across sectarian lines, not to the point of visiting in each other's homes, which would be dangerous, but to meeting in neutral areas.

The Peace People is another organization that sends groups of teenagers out of the country each summer on peace and reconciliation trips. The first time I met Charlie Cooper from Ballyfergus he was talking with a group of youngsters at Fredheim House who would be going to Norway. He was laying it on the line.

"This is not a holiday," he warned them. "It's hard work. There will be intensive encounter sessions. You can expect to shed some tears as the barriers start to come down. It can be painful."

There would be thirty-nine of them, sixteen- and seventeen-year-olds, plus five counselors—somewhat older than the groups that go to the United States with Channels of Peace. The plan is to stay for a week in a camp by a lake in the country; the second week they'd live in town with host families but get together daily. "It would be better to keep them at the camp the whole time. Then they're a captive audience," Charlie said. "But that costs money. It's less intense when they stay with host families, but it doesn't cost us anything."

"Norwegians have different expectations of young people," he told them. "There will be *no drinking* for two weeks. Not even a glass of wine with dinner, even if the host family offers it. Nothing! You break that rule and home you go, no discussion. You'll ruin it for yourself, but you'll also ruin it for other people in the future."

Drugs are not a problem in Northern Ireland, but teenage drinking is, as it is for all age groups. The legal drinking age is eighteen; in the South, someone told me, bartenders will serve underage drinkers because of the economic depression—a customer is a customer. But laws are tougher in Northern Ireland, and young drinkers get someone of legal age to make their purchases for them.

Not all of the peace projects work well. Carleen told me about a group that was stuck in a castle outside a small country town on the continent. Isolated and bored, they got into minor trouble. The police appeared frequently at the castle gates, which shocked the kids. "Here, the police come only when somebody's been killed," Carleen said. Finally the "peace and reconciliation" group was sent home.

Carleen was busy that day setting up contacts for a newspaper editor from Iowa who wanted to meet all the important political figures in Northern Ireland—like Ian Paisley. "It's very hard to do," she said. "They're all busy people, and it takes at least ten phone calls to line up each one." Nevertheless, that seemed to be the kind of treatment foreign journalists expect.

"Tomorrow a Spanish TV crew is coming to interview some of our young people," she said. "Maybe you'd like to come back to watch."

The Media

Journalists are not liked in Northern Ireland. In the worst view they are seen as parasites and scavengers who live off the misery of others. At best they are seen as uninformed and uninterested in the people they're reporting; they want to get their stories and run. "They spend an hour here to write a newspaper article, a day to write a magazine article, a week to write a book," someone complained to me. And someone else said, "Most of the articles about Northern Ireland are written at the bar at the Forum."

The Forum Hotel is the best—and the best known—of Belfast's hotels, a modern building with a luxurious lobby in the city center. It's the place most foreign journalists and media people and well-heeled tourists stay. Previously named the Europa, it was bombed twenty-nine times—a no-fail method used by terrorists to catch media attention, since the media were already there, drinking in the bar and eating in the dining room. Now it is surrounded by a security fence, and people going in and out must pass through a little wooden building with security officers who make a quick check or none at all.

One evening I strolled through the Forum listening for American accents. It didn't take long to find them. A group of lawyers were on a ten-day "fact-finding tour" of Northern Ireland, shepherded by a Dublin-born journalist based in Boston. They moved as a pack like schoolchildren on a class outing from one expensive hotel to the next, following a carefully prescribed itinerary that was supposed to give them political insight. They thought I was crazy to be traveling alone in Northern Ireland or anywhere else. I thought they were crazier to be in a group; it's not a good way to learn about a place.

On another evening I met a man and woman who were producing a program for American television. New Yorkers traveling on a hefty expense account, they were in Belfast for a few days doing preliminary research on their project: a documentary focusing on teenagers born in 1969, the year the Troubles began. They were concerned exclusively with kids in trouble—the joy-riding, glue-sniffing, rock-throwing, petrol-bombing, cop-baiting, hell-raising fringe. I had found many other young people doing many other things instead: going off on holiday schemes, singing in choruses, taking exams, judging pigs, signing up for the Bru, falling in love, looking for jobs, worrying about the future. I thought the New York TV people should put a notice at the beginning and at the end of their documentary: WARNING—THIS REPRESENTS ONLY A SMALL PERCENTAGE OF THE YOUTH OF NORTHERN IRELAND.

Obviously I didn't offer this suggestion, didn't comment that in my opinion they were misrepresenting the facts, distorting the truth. But they made it pretty clear they thought that in my search for a variety of voices in Northern Ireland, I was missing out on the hot news.

By contrast, I was impressed with the way the Spaniards went about their project. London-based correspondents for Spanish television, they were producing a forty-five-minute special on Northern Ireland. They had been meeting with political and church leaders, and now they were prepared to spend an hour with Youth for Peace, part of the Community of the Peace People.

The young people who had been asked to come for the dialogue sat around for an hour waiting, getting increasingly tense and jittery. But once the crew arrived in a white Mercedes station wagon driven by a local TV producer, things moved quickly. In no time a few lights had been set up and the group of a dozen or so settled down around the group leader, Leo. A rangy, curly-haired, part-time student at Queen's, Leo has been a member of Peace People for all of its ten-year existence, since he was twelve years old.

The reporter's suggestion that the peace movement was dying produced fierce replies that it is still very much alive and even growing slowly, although there are no more peace rallies.

"*Our* lives have been affected," a young man with a mustache said fervently. "I grew up in a relatively unbigoted Protestant family, but I was hounded in school for having Catholic friends. There's no way I could ever bring up my children to be bigoted."

A girl named Maeve had dressed for her TV appearance in a snug white sleeveless summer dress, although it could not have been more than fifty degrees outside. When someone else talked about being shunned by friends for their involvement with the peace movement, Maeve said that she's also a Republican, but the Sinn Fein (the political arm of the IRA) sees her as a Peace Person, and the Peace People see her as a Sinn Feiner. And when someone mentioned the RUC, Maeve jumped into that one too, describing how the police stopped her to check her driver's license.

"Prods get polite treatment, 'yessir, good evening sir, may I see your license if you don't mind sir,' but if you're Catholic they're *rude*. It was cold and raining the night they stopped me, but they made me stand out in the pouring rain for fifteen minutes while they searched the car, and I didn't even have a coat with me. Just let me stand there shivering, and never a word of apology."

When the camera had been turned off and the lights killed, the Spanish producer told them that he saw many similarities between Northern Ireland and South Africa, where he had been on a recent assignment. That brought me into the conversation, but in an odd way. They were talking about censorship, particularly the blatant form of it practiced in South Africa, when suddenly one of the boys turned to me.

"American TV is dishonest!" he said. "They take old footage, stuff made in 1969, in 1972, and they show it as part of a newscast and say that it's current news." I said they surely identified it as file material, but he was adamant and angry. For all the faults I could find with American broadcast journalists, that particular form of deceit was not one of them.

"The French are worse," someone said. "A French TV crew actually paid kids to start throwing rocks, to provoke an incident, and then they filmed it." I had heard the same story in South Africa, but there it was the *American* crew that made the payoff. And always I wonder how much truth there is to these tales of reporters who are not content to report the facts.

The Spaniard asked the question I always seemed to be asking: what about your future? Everyone in the group was determined to stay in the country, but it was Maeve in the white dress who said wistfully, "The only reason I'd leave is because of a job. This could be a wonderful place to live."

XII

BELFAST:
TAKE TWO. TAKE THREE.

A free day, no appointments, no place in particular I was supposed to be. I had learned to find my way around Belfast. I was winding down at the end of my trip. The weather was gentler, friendlier than it had been, a perfect day for people-watching.

In the city center people basked in the watery sunshine, lining up for cones of soft ice cream dispensed from a machine parked by the door of a food shop. Buskers—street musicians—were out in force, their territories staked out, their instrument cases open for donations while they sang and played guitars, saxophones, mandolins. I noticed, not for the first time, that the women of Northern Ireland seem indifferent to fashion—there is none of the elegance on the streets of Belfast that you'd find in London, for instance. The young go in for punk and funk: a girl sauntered by in tight, eye-searing, orange pants and shirt with black polka dots the size of saucers, her hair dyed a matching shade of orange.

In a wooden gazebo in the middle of the pedestrian mall a group of dancers in oversize shirts and tight pants stepped precisely through their routine to rock music while a TV camera rolled. A small crowd gathered to watch, licking their ice cream. Take one. Take two. Take three.

I stopped by the Northern Ireland Tourist Board to thank some people who had been helpful to me. The security in that building was unusually strict—not because of the Tourist Board, as it turned out, but because RUC has some administrative offices there. One of the guards at the entrance checked my bag; then he rang upstairs for someone to come to the lobby and escort me. "You've been here before," he said.

"A couple of times," I admitted.

"I thought I recognized you," he said. "You or your Russian accent."

That was a joke; we all laughed.

"So what's your impression of Northern Ireland?" asked the other.

"It's a beautiful country," I said.

"Here visiting relations?"

"No. As far as I know, I don't have a drop of Irish blood in my veins."

"And aren't you bloody lucky for that!" he exclaimed.

I think that was a joke too. At any rate, we all laughed again.

I found a record shop and browsed through the bins, looking for tapes by Phil Coulter, the musician who wrote "The Town I Loved So Well." His music was filed under "Traditional and Irish Folk," along with a singing group called the Wolfe Tones, named for the eighteenth century patriot. There was another bin labeled "12th of July" with Orange marching bands playing Orange favorites.

But I was more interested in the other customers than I

was in the albums. Especially the punks. One had shaved the sides of his head and dyed his mohawk bright fuchsia. His buddy with hair the color of marigolds gelled into spikes sported a nose bead, earrings, multiple chains with multiple crosses, a wrist full of thin silver bracelets, tall black leather boots crisscrossed with straps. Outside on the mall a dozen similarly dressed individuals lounged on the pavement in front of a shop, mostly in black leather with lots of metal studs. I caught the eye of a young RUC man in a bulletproof vest also enjoying the sunshine, and I asked him how the shopowners put up with this goofy-looking bunch on their doorsteps. There were no laws against loitering, the policeman said, and unless they got unruly, they were allowed to stay.

"We all have our odd little ways, now don't we?" he asked philosophically and sauntered off.

Back in the university area, I browsed through a bookstore, where Bob Geldof's autobiography was prominently displayed with "Sir Bob!" tags attached; it had been announced the day before that the rock star had been named to honorary knighthood. His drive to help African famine victims had raised more than a hundred million dollars at Live-Aid rock concerts in 1985 and a global Sport-Aid extravaganza in May. The flap of his book, *Is That All?*, warned that many parents might object to the contents.

The Student Union of Queen's University, Belfast, was around the corner. I stopped in to visit the restroom, although it certainly wasn't necessary to go out of my way to find one. There are plenty of public toilets throughout Northern Ireland—nicely kept ones, too, with shining white tile and polished brass handrails and doorknobs. And they are called *toilets*—not restrooms, or powder rooms, or ladies' rooms, and certainly not bathrooms (which is where one takes a bath), or by any other euphemism. This directness catches Americans off-guard. People ask, "Do you want to use the toilet?" although some more Victorian types go completely around the bend and ask, "Do you want to wash your hands?"

I went into the toilet in the Student Union not to wash my hands but to check the graffiti. In addition to the usual lesbian *vs.* straight debates and the usual (in Northern Ireland) political slogans, there were some interesting variations, "Ulster says NO—but the man from Del Monte, he say YES!" was a reference to a TV commercial for Del Monte brand pineapple. Under the pious and patriotic "God Save the Queen," someone had scribbled "Why? What did that silly old bat ever do for you?" And my favorite of the comments on male/female relations, this cynical observation: "First you sink in his arms—then your arms are in his sink."

As I walked toward Miss Drumm's, admiring the architectural detail of the old brick houses that only a few weeks before had seemed so dull and dreary, I realized that I had mellowed out a lot in my attitude toward Northern Ireland. Maybe the change in the weather had something to do with it. Maybe my feelings toward a few special people had even more to do with it.

Good-byes to Old Friends

"I thought you'd be hungry for some food with *taste* to it," Trevor Hand, the journalist, said, and told me we were going to an Indian restaurant for dinner. We met outside Trevor's office. We had not seen each other in over a month, not since the first time we had met during my first couple of days in Northern Ireland. He had helped me then with lists of people he thought I should know, places I should go, things I should watch for. And now he wanted to share a meal, one with some taste to it, and hear about my adventures.

I didn't wait until we got to the restaurant but launched immediately into stories about "Stroke City" and other places and anecdotes about the people I met there. He watched me with some amusement while I chattered on and on. The ideas he had offered me had led in other directions to still more ideas. "I wouldn't be at all surprised," he said, "if you found an Indian restaurant that's better than this one, too."

Living in the southwestern United States, I have acquired a taste for spicy food, and I ordered up the hottest dish I could find on the menu. It still seemed tame. "There is no *cuisine* here, as there is in European countries," Trevor complained. "In Italy, for instance, even simple food is cuisine. People care about food in Italy and France and Spain. Nobody cares about food here. It's boring."

I had noticed that. As long as the meat was cooked to death and there were plenty of chips, everybody was happy. Once I had been invited for a Sunday dinner. We ate plain boiled chicken with mashed potatoes and roast potatoes and not a green vegetable in sight.

After dinner we went to a comic concert where the musicians clowned outrageously. Some of the clowning was quite good, technically demanding, but I was surprised at the content: a lot of the humor was based on heavy drinking. The audience howled. At intermission I mentioned that drunkenness wasn't often a subject of comedy in the United States any more; people no longer laughed at the drunk stumbling across the stage or leaning tipsily against a lamppost. Trevor's eyebrows arched. "Really? You don't say!" An interesting reaction from a man who had invested a considerable amount of time investigating the devastating effects of alcoholism on his country.

On the way back to Miss Drumm's, we stopped off at a pub on the corner. The bar was filled with middle-aged men getting drearily drunk. One of them was humming to himself, pretending he was Zorba the Greek, executing a wavering little dance step. The television blared, but only a few people were watching—or even staring at it. Most of the others gazed morosely into their pints of Guinness. It was a depressing place.

The TV news came on, mostly sports. The previous night the soccer team from Northern Ireland had played Brazil in the World Cup play-offs in Mexico. They were defeated, 3–0, as everyone predicted, but national pride was nevertheless running high. "Think of the determination!" crowed Trevor. "A little country like this, producing champions! The British are afraid of getting their uniforms dirty, of scratching their knees. That determination to survive is typical of Northern Ireland."

Outside Miss Drumm's we said good-bye and good luck and promised to keep in touch, and then we shook hands formally and went our separate ways.

Handshaking, I found, was about as much physical contact as the people of Ulster can take, as much affection as they are comfortable displaying. When I first began spending time with Seamus and Bridie McHugh, participating in their family get-togethers, I quickly developed a real affection for them. They had become a kind of surrogate family for me, providing a warm base that I needed. And I behaved with them the way I behave with my own family—I hugged them. That was a mistake. I could feel Seamus tense up when I threw my arms around him, and I didn't do it again.

I asked Father Paul about the no-touch rule during one of our long, philosophical conversations. "The Irish are not a tactile people," he said. "When I counsel couples who come to me before they're married, I try to tell them that touching and hugging are *good*. Things like holding hands are important." He was not one to talk; when I said good-bye to him and hugged him, he tensed up, too.

I never really quit trying with those people I came to care about, but when the reaction was a stiff one, I backed off. Nevertheless something changed in the few weeks I had known Bridie and Seamus. I spent my last night in Northern Ireland with them; the next day I would be on a bumpy bus to Galway, the first leg of my trip home.

It was Seamus who made the move, grabbing me in a fierce embrace, Bridie right behind him.

EPILOGUE:
GETTING IT STRAIGHT

The Reporter

He writes for the newspaper in one of the small towns I visited, and he came around to interview "the American author." That gave me a chance to interview *him*. We found an empty office and shut the door. The reporter asked me some questions, I asked him some, but mostly we talked. And talked and talked.

The reporter is a short, dark man. Playing the usual game of guessing which foot he digs with, I would have said Catholic—and I would have been wrong.

"I'm a Protestant," he said, "with a Catholic first name and a Scottish surname. A few years ago I married a Catholic woman, and now we have a child. A few years ago I was a true Orangie. My blood would begin to bubble at the start of the marching season, come to a boil on the Twelfth of July, simmer down again by the sixteenth. I'd put on my black bowler and my orange sash and be out there with the rest of them. I dreamed of the day my child would be part of that, and proud of that Protestant heritage."

And then what happened?

He put away his notebook. "Call it Christianity," he said.

I remarked that I hadn't heard that word, or that concept, referred to much in Northern Ireland. Most of what happened in this country between Catholics and Protestants seems a perversion of what I understand to be Christianity.

"People like to say that the Orange Order has to do with tradition," the reporter said. "It doesn't. It has to do with power. All that marching—that's just bravado, to show the Catholics who's boss, who's on top. I don't want any part of that any more."

Why had he married a Catholic, if he had been such a strong Orangeman?

"I think it may have been an insidious way of striking a blow at the Papists, by taking one of theirs. I don't even like to think about it any more."

"How did she deal with your bigotry?"

"Somehow she allowed it. She's a better person than I am. But she's glad I'm over it."

We talked then about the impossibility of compromise in Northern Ireland because of the fear of change. Both sides —whether you call them Catholic and Protestant or Nationalist and Unionist or Republican and Loyalist—are extremely conservative, very right-wing. The economic situation would make a drift to the left seem natural, but the people totally mistrust anything that smacks of socialism. "For every solution, Ulster comes up with another problem."

I told him that I found the people of this country wonderfully cordial and hospitable—to strangers like me—but lacking in *charity*, in love for one another. And I told him I thought the whole country was neurotically depressed. "Depression hangs like a black cloud over everything," I said. "And everyone is affected, whether they recognize it or not. There might not be terrorists on every street corner, but there is tension everywhere. I think that's worse."

He had another appointment then, and so did I. "I owe you an apology," he said as we were leaving. "I was very cynical about meeting you—another American writer coming to tell us what's wrong with our country. We're a stubborn, insular breed, and we don't take kindly to being told how to solve the problem by people who have had only five minutes' experience of a situation that has arisen over hundreds of years. I don't know how you did it, but you really do understand the situation here."

I am not an expert on Northern Ireland, that doesn't happen in a matter of weeks. But his words gave me the reassurance I needed that I was on target. I was sorry I hadn't known him long enough to hug him.

The Poet

The poet is a heavyset young woman of twenty-two who looks middle-aged, her long, ginger-colored hair pulled back in a single braid, glasses slipping on her prominent nose. She has been writing poetry since she was fifteen, maybe younger, collecting it in neat notebooks, her rounded handwriting careful but her grammar and spelling unsure.

The poet is the eldest of several children. She was five years old in 1969 when the Troubles began. Her parents both worked, and she went to stay with her grandparents in a rural village that is about half Protestant, half Catholic. The poet is Catholic.

When she finished high school she went to technical school to learn child care, but the government reduced its support to agencies that might have hired her, and she could not get a job. She went on the Bru, living so frugally that she was able to save enough money to buy the cottage where she and her grandparents live, a tiny, primitive place without running water or indoor plumbing but a magnificent view of Lough Neagh in the distance. "Gran is eighty-five, a Donegal woman, full of life," she said. "Gran-Da is seventy-nine, an Armagh man, so he can keep up with her."

But the poet's life has changed. With a government employment scheme that pays her salary for a year, she was hired by a community organization to start a youth club in her village. Now she's busy with her youth club—it's supposed to be mixed, but it's predominantly Catholic—taking one trip after another to places she has never been before, like Dublin. Gran gets so depressed without her that she refuses to eat while her granddaughter is gone.

Worse than that, the youth work takes time away from the poet's writing, and it's her writing that defines who she is. Always there is the struggle to find the time for her work, and to find the words she needs. In a few weeks, when the Protestant marching season would make life miserable for Catholics, she planned to go to Spain for a vacation with her sister and a friend. It would be her first trip off the island. She'll take her pen and notebook, and while the others are sight-seeing or lounging around the pool, she will be in her room, writing.

Mostly she writes about Ulster and about the Troubles. She's never been *directly* affected, she says; that is, no one in her family has been killed. But she talks about the insistent throb of helicopters flying low overhead at 6:00 A.M., the rattle of machine-gun fire, the muffled thump of bombs exploding. She remembers with a shudder the day of the Loyalist strike in a nearby town last spring: masked men were everywhere, tractors belonging to local farmers used to block off the center of town. No matter which direction she turned, her way was blocked. She was terrified, until an uncle spotted her and yanked her to safety.

Hardly anyone knows about her poems. Her goal in her poetry, she said, is to be "always more powerful." She's aware of her lack of technique, and the few people to whom she has shown her work have criticized it for lack of rhyme and meter. "But I'm mostly interested in a short, powerful statement of my ideas and feelings," she said. It hasn't occurred to her to submit her work for publication; that's not important—not yet.

Shyly, the poet offered me her poems. She calls it "rough work," still needing revision, further polishing. One of them really touched me. "You can have it," she said, half-proud, half-apologetic. "Use it, if you like it."

I copied it into my own notebook. The best part is here—in these last four lines:

Ulster speaks
But is never listened to.
It yearns for peace
And waits.

October 3, 1986
Albuquerque, New Mexico

FURTHER READING

Nonfiction

Children in Conflict. Morris Fraser (New York: Basic Books, 1973)

Children of War. Roger Rosenblatt (London: New English Library, 1983)

Ireland: A Terrible Beauty. Jill and Leon Uris (New York: Doubleday, 1975)

The Irish. Thomas J. O'Hanlon (London: Deutsch, 1976)

Northern Ireland: Captive of History. Gary MacEoin (New York: Holt, Rinehart & Winston, 1974)

The Political Life of Children. Robert Coles (Boston: Atlantic Monthly, 1986)

The Price of My Soul. Bernadette Devlin (New York: Knopf, 1969)

Too Long a Sacrifice: Life and Death in Northern Ireland since 1969. Jack Holland (New York: Dodd, Mead, 1981)

Fiction and Poetry

The Collected Poems of W. B. Yeats. William Butler Yeats (New York: Macmillan, 1933)

Dubliners. James Joyce (New York: Penguin Books, 1976)

Field Work. Seamus Heaney (New York: Farrar, Straus, Giroux, 1979)

Nothing Happens in Carmincross. Benedict Kiely (Boston: David R. Godine, 1985)

Trinity. Leon Uris (New York: Doubleday, 1976)

INDEX

INDEX